Deschutes
Public Library

D1023532

the pop classics series

most dramatic ever.

the bachelor

suzannah showler

ecwpress

Copyright © Suzannah Showler, 2018

Published by ECW Press
665 Gerrard Street East
Toronto, Ontario, Canada M4M 1Y2
416-694-3348 / info@ecwpress.com

All rights reserved. No part of this publication
may be reproduced, stored in a retrieval
system, or transmitted in any form by
any process — electronic, mechanical,
photocopying, recording, or otherwise
— without the prior written permission of
the copyright owners and ECW Press. The
scanning, uploading, and distribution of this
book via the Internet or via any other means
without the permission of the publisher is illegal
and punishable by law. Please purchase only
authorized electronic editions, and do not
participate in or encourage electronic piracy
of copyrighted materials. Your support of the
author's rights is appreciated.

Editors for the press:
Crissy Calhoun and Jennifer Knoch
Cover and text design: David Gee
Series proofreader: Avril McMeekin

Library and Archives Canada
Cataloguing in Publication

Showler, Suzannah, author
Most dramatic ever : The bachelor /
Suzannah Showler.

(Pop classics ; 9)
Includes bibliographical references.
Issued in print and electronic formats.
ISBN 978-1-77041-392-4 (softcover)
Also issued as: 978-1-77305-168-0 (PDF)
ISBN 978-1-77305-167-3 (ePUB)

1. Bachelor (Television program).
2. Bachelorette (Television program).
3. Dating shows (Television programs)—
Social aspects—United States.
4. Reality television programs—Social
aspects—United States. I. Title.
II. Series: Pop classic series ; 9

PN1992.77.B245S56 2018   791.45'72
C2017-906222-0   C2017-906223-9

Printing: Norecob   5   4   3   2   1
PRINTED AND BOUND IN CANADA

The publication of *Most Dramatic Ever* has been generously supported by the Government of
Canada through the Canada Book Fund. *Ce livre est financé en partie par le gouvernement
du Canada.* We also acknowledge the contribution of the Government of Ontario through the
Ontario Book Publishing Tax Credit and the Ontario Media Development Corporation.

Contents

Introduction: Most Dramatic Ever

It's a swimming pool at the edge of the world. The far lip of the pool juts over a vast coastal panorama as if the steep drop-off to the ocean happens here, maybe right under our feet. Everything is water and light and water: the up-close, unreal blue of the pool picked up in the ocean, which takes the color and runs with it, bolting towards the horizon at the speed of a shimmer, colliding with the preposterous, unbroken blue of the sky. It's impossible to say which part — man-made or natural — is the imitation. It all seems like one thing.

This is the first shot of the first episode of *The Bachelor*. It's brief, just a few moments, but the beauty it shows is willful, boggling, engineered for optical illusion. Even if you've never been to California, you know this is California. The way every element — pool, ocean, sky — flattens with an eager camera-readiness makes you think maybe people build mansions and pools in places like this not to look at the view, but to be inside it. And the mistake of thinking the ground drops out from under us — maybe that's the idea. Maybe it's kind of true. Like there are places where the whole point of beauty, of nature, is to condition us to get something wrong.

It's just a few seconds. The camera swings left, and standing on the pool deck there's a man in a summer suit that looks like millennium-era Gap khaki taking a crack at formalwear. "Hi," he says, "I'm Chris Harrison. And no, I'm not the Bachelor."

When *The Bachelor* debuted in 2002, it was hardly a latecomer to the reality TV party, but it also wasn't leading the vanguard. In summer 2000, when *Survivor* — with its safe, silly contrivance overlaid with the dark exposure of bare life — turned out to be an explosive ratings-gobbler, it appeared that something about the palate of 21st-century TV viewers had either exposed itself or been whetted. In the glut of turn-of-the-millennium reality TV that followed, *The Bachelor* was solidly in the middle: after *Big Brother* and *Fear Factor*, before *America's Next Top Model* and *The Simple Life*, in just about the same breath as *American Idol*.

By virtue of its subject (hetero dating), *The Bachelor* also has ancestral roots reaching back to the 1960s and '70s with *The Dating Game*: that game show classic where bachelors numbered one through three (sometimes gender-reversed) compete with ice-breaking trivia for a chance to take a prize woman out on the studio's dime. *The Dating Game* ran for a decade in the mid-'60s and then, like the matchmaking undead, was revived three times between the late '70s and late '90s. Without the seriality of *The Bachelor*, *Dating* was pure game show, suffering no fuss over "reasons," right or wrong, to sign up as a contestant. A common gig for struggling actors, *Dating Game* archives are a real treasure trove of before-they-were-famous footage.

There are also *Bachelor* relations among its own reality cohort, kissing cousins (maybe more like drunk makeout cousins?) like *Blind Date* and *Temptation Island*. *Blind Date*, which ran from 1999 into the mid-aughts, set couples up on multi-part, multi-drink dates then glossed the footage — often pretty dull on its face — with cheeky cartoon thought bubbles. *Temptation Island* was a kind of false rumspringa, bringing four committed couples to a resort, splitting them up, and surrounding each with a cast of (tempting, hence the name) professional bods of the opposite sex. *Temptation* was sort of *The Bachelor*'s inverse — an experiment in romance-busting rather than building — but tapped the same fears and longings. In its own way, it held up monogamy as an aspirational, self-improving end.

Finally, the closest comp by virtue of its shared paternity is *Bachelor* executive producer Mike Fleiss's first televised matrimonial extravaganza, *Who Wants to Marry a Multi-Millionaire?* — *Homo habilis* to *The Bachelor*'s *erectus*. A single two-hour special aired in 2000, *Millionaire* was a classic, 50-state American beauty pageant with a shadowy sugar daddy (literally: he was only visible in silhouette) serving as both judge and winner's crown (no "scholarship program" here). Twenty-two million people tuned in to watch Miss-turned-Mrs. Millionaire claim her prize of on-the-spot wedlock to the moneybags. Just as soon as the couple had honeymooned-slash-met, it was revealed that FOX had done poor vetting on their "millionaire next door" (as Fleiss had called him), who had a restraining order from an ex-fiancée on the grounds of domestic violence. He'd also fudged his professional creds, his name, and quite possibly the barely plural millions for which he'd been cast. Whoopsie-daisy! Better background checks next time.

Despite this unalloyed failure, Fleiss remained convinced that America was thirsty for reality TV–made marriage. (After all, 22 million had tuned in to watch his wayward liability pageant in the first place.) After striking out at a couple of other networks, Fleiss sold ABC on another show about dozens of women pursuing a single man's hand. This time the pitch was less beauty pageant and more true love on crack: the usual beats, from meet-cute to matrimony, cranked up by the presence of rivals and the fantasy-making efforts of TV production. A competitive fairy tale. *The Bachelor* was signed for six one-hour episodes and given an eight-week, shoestring shoot in which to make Mike Fleiss's dreams come true. It was, for Fleiss, a second chance at (producing) love.

Unscripted dating shows that came before *The Bachelor* generated the standard reality TV goodies: embarrassing moments, interpersonal drama, the ups and downs of competition. But they had a common failing: prodding at schadenfreude under the auspices of dating made dating look bad. Though these shows were allegedly about romance, none was actually *romantic*.

So, yeah, uh, *The Bachelor* doesn't really have that problem. A many-candle-lined, rose-petal-strewn, sunset-lit journey to find The One, the *Bachelor*'s romance is pitched to take your breath away, suck oxygen, smother. The show has never been coy about its ambitions. In the very first episode, Chris Harrison tells us: "This is not an ordinary relationship show — the stakes are considerably higher here. This is about something real. Something permanent. You know, the whole till death do you part thing?"

It may have been joining the spate of crass human spectacles hurled up in TV to ring in the 21st century, but *The Bachelor* parades shamelessly into lofty rhetoric past centuries have left to their poets. From the beginning, the show asserted its right not to choose between high and low, professing to expose the drama of real people acting out of loneliness and fear, then pull it together for the payoff of happily ever after. And with this blunt promise, *The Bachelor* reassured viewers that it was okay for us to want it both ways.

At its beating, rose-red heart, *The Bachelor* is basically just two things: it's a game show, and it's a love story — more particularly, a marriage plot. And before you think about it too hard, the pairing sounds so natural that it's hard to believe someone even had to think it up. Like, wait, was that not already a thing? After all, the game show and the marriage plot are, arguably, the defining innovations of middle-class entertainment of the 20th and 18th-into-19th centuries, respectively. Both genres are so endlessly popular and endlessly replicable that the twain shall meet seems more like a command than a proposition. *The Bachelor* as inevitability.

But if public competition meets love-'n'-marriage Romance sounds like a harmonious populist twinning, the moment you think it through it's obvious the genres ought to be mutually exclusive. Though both game shows and love stories offer a fantasy of delivery from regular life, they propose that different forces compel the ascent. The game show publicizes the ordinary individual as a competitor who channels luck and skill to author their own fate. The marriage plot reveals that even the ordinary individual may be chosen and moved by the benevolent authority of a fate beyond their control. So on the one hand, *The Bachelor* is a competition, and it's anyone's game. On the other hand, it also purports to be an expression of romantic destiny: a series of turns plotted to reach a preordained end.

That illogic isn't a bug — it's a feature. In fact, it's the very crux of *The Bachelor*'s tenacious, addictive endurance. Because in its refusal to choose between a game show's effort and a love story's kismet, I argue that *The Bachelor* is the ultimate specimen of American entertainment, mimicking a similar refusal to choose between foundational myths at the heart of the nation's identity and self-image. The show presents as an open playing field, freely available for any individual to enter, meet, and conquer. Then when someone actually wins, their victory is recast as the inexorable allotment of fortune.

Differently put: for weeks the show dramatizes the pursuit of individual happiness, only to claim in the end that it was manifesting destiny all along. And so *The Bachelor* delivers that oxymoronic, impossibly American dream of working hard for your innate exceptionalism, of pulling yourself up by the boot straps to step into your fate.

In the beginning, the show sent out Chris Harrison to assure us that this wasn't just fun and games. And yet it still needed to deliver a Bachelor for whom 25 women would be inspired to compete. The Bachelor could not merely be eligible — he needed to be a prize.

The first Bachelor, Alex Michel, was, believe it or not, a pedigreed brain. As though lifted straight from a '90s teen flick, the photo montage of his life narrated by Harrison shows a dork rescued by "contact lenses and countless hours in the swimming pool," achieving homecoming popularity and varsity athleti- cism, and then whipping those specs back out to give his vale- dictory address. With a lit degree from Harvard and Stanford business school for postgrad, Michel's résumé hinted at erudite sensitivity but management salary. Having plucked him out of thin air, the show confirmed the Bachelor as a worthwhile love object using real-world indicators of status.[1]

For a few rounds in its shakier middle years, *The Bachelor*

---

1 Similarly, when Chris Harrison sits down to brief Alex, the very first thing he reports about the Bachelor's dating pool is that it contains two doctors, two lawyers, and ten women with graduate degrees. Let's just say it was a very different *Bachelor* world.

would, as it did that first season, foray into the real world to drum up a lead, trying on a different variation of prestige each time. Between 2004 and 2008, the spread of Bachelors included the silver-spooned heir to an all-American fortune (Andrew Firestone, of the tires), a naval officer (crisp uniform at the ready, natch), a pro football player (who could barely keep his dates' names straight, but we didn't know as much about concussions back then), a pseudo-royal, a pseudo-celebrity (actor Charlie O'Connell, lesser brother of Jerry), and a posh-sounding Brit.

Staggered between these representatives of real-life cachet were leads cast from within the franchise's own universe. With the introduction of *The Bachelorette* in 2003, led by Trista Rehn, runner-up from the inaugural *Bachelor* season, the show established a tradition of selecting a love object from among the previous season's final rejects. This was sometimes the case for *The Bachelor* (in all but the examples mentioned above), and always for *The Bachelorette*. After a while, when reaching sporadically into the world at large didn't turn up anything all that great anyway, the show gave up on taking in leads from outside the *Bachelor* mansion altogether. Since 2009, every Bachelor and Bachelorette has been an internal hire.

As a result, the criteria the show holds up as exemplary of Bachelorhood — and, by extension, marriageability — have changed. Turning away from education, class, and other line-items of societal value, the worth of the lead is now established through the only currency that changes hands within *Bachelor* society itself: love and its loss. Being elevated to love object is a salve to the wound the show itself inflicts. You earn true love by getting dumped on TV.

The world *The Bachelor* has built as the staging ground for its love stories is particularly and fundamentally cruel. This isn't an agnostic roll through the win some, lose some bingo tumbler of real-life romance: it's a goal-oriented pilgrimage with a rigorously enforced quota of repercussive pain. Everyone but the hero or heroine and their beloved — that earned-but-chosen one and only — is collateral.

To be real, what we're talking about here is a kind of religion: The *Bachelor* universe is patterned by the simplicity of sacrifice's call and redemption's answer. That reliable toggle from *Bachelor* to *Bachelorette* and back again is essentially Christian morality with all the bennies of reincarnation. From our god's-eye view in front of the screen, we follow the broken into their next life, bear witness to their rebirth and reward. Culling its heroes and heroines from those felled in the name of the journey, the show chugs onward, giving the audience permission to believe that our voyeurism is useful. Without all the pain and drama we are hungry to witness, there would be no love stories to tell.

TV is the medium of repetition. This has not stopped being true as TV has gone prestige. It has not even stopped being true (yet) as streaming services have transformed what kinds of shows can be tried out, gambled on, and produced. Even through wide-scale developments in what is made and of what quality, television has not shaken its deep bond with reliability. To be a viewer of a TV show is to be a repeat customer at the trough of a feeling.

If this aphorism holds any weight, *The Bachelor* is the most TV of them all. It's been around for a donkey's age, and in 16 years — 22 seasons of *The Bachelor* and 13 of *The Bachelorette* — the show's format has changed practically not at all. Rather, it has doubled down, taken its tendencies and codified them into rules, sanctifying its inaugural accidents and impulses as traditional.

And it's not in spite of this conservative urge but because of it that *The Bachelor* has become more relevant over time rather than less. Which brings me to another of *The Bachelor*'s contradictions: it's both a relic and a prophet — a time-traveler from first-gen reality TV that would prove itself a harbinger of Tinder. Its format has come to mirror realities its audience (which skews young, aging at a slower rate than the show itself) will find familiar. A smorgasbord of bullet-point prospective partners isn't so different from swiping left and right. And the aggressive surveillance of reality TV is only an exaggerated version of something most of us have learned to live with and which many — particularly but not only those who were raised with it — have embraced as a means of tweaking, filtering, and even *making* a sense of self.

The Bachelor secures contemporary relevance not only in what it says, but in how it says it. The show has a dialect, a *Bachelor*-speak that is both internally consistent season to season and crucial to the show's moments of highest drama.

Contestants vie for the commodity of "one-on-one time" in which they might develop "a connection" with the Bachelor. This connection is confirmed by "the rose." The greatest threat to the Bachelor's "journey to find love" is the production-ensured inevitability that some of the competing contestants are not "there for the right reasons." The *Bachelor* vernacular speaks directly to what have grown into the dominant anxieties of contemporary social life in general, and romance in particular: the fear that our connections are inauthentic, our gestures empty, our socially mediated lives at once overcrowded and isolated. In *The Bachelor*'s case, TV stayed the same — it's reality that changed.

The threat posed by unscripted TV shows in the era of *The Bachelor*'s conception — that reality itself might suffer by virtue of having been uttered in the same breath as television — seems quaint and folksy now, like a cute story about terrified Parisians leaping out of the path of the Lumière Brothers' train.

We're all veterans of reality TV. From factory farm to table, we know all the gory steps by which the sausage gets to our plates. And we don't really care. We maybe even love it more. It's not unlike appreciating a sonnet for its rhythm and rhyme: you don't have to pretend that a poet thinks in iambs in order for their work to mean something to you.

In fact, in the case of *The Bachelor*, I'll go so far as to say that a kind of realism has become integral to the romantic flight of fancy. Understanding the conditions under which the show is manufactured has only served to confirm that the thing the show aims to cultivate — what Chris Harrison in the first episode calls "one of the most wonderful things love has to offer: marriage, but with love and romance" — is resilient, will bloom in even the most constrained, scrutinized, and contrived circumstances. Viewers remain safely on the inside of the joke, aware of the preposterousness of the situation while also allowing ourselves to be carried away by its results. It's a form of emotional engineering so effective it seems to work on an almost cellular level — the entertainment value equivalent of a Cheeto's ability to disappear when it hits your tongue, leaving you with all the caloric intake but still hungry for more, certain you've consumed only air.

Being given permission to toggle between contradictions is insanely powerful. It's addictive. And even as it gets us hooked, *The Bachelor* lets viewers feel like we're empowered to look at the picture in front of us and decide for ourselves which elements are man-made and which are natural — what is camera-ready performance, what is real emotion.

Which begs the question: what does it even mean for a feeling to be real? With its burlesque of real life, *The Bachelor* suggests something about the role performance plays in the production of all romance. Sure, *The Bachelor* may be absurd, but so is falling in love anywhere, with anyone. Even more ludicrous is the fact that we've lugged a mercantile tradition for exchanging women as goods into the 21st century and made it an object of worship. (I'm very happily married, by the way.) The tension between the lofty rhetoric of romance and the banal pragmatism of marriage is something we live with in every part of our culture, not just on TV. Romance is a story; marriage is a contract.

No matter what *The Bachelor* may say, the truth is there are no right reasons to go on a reality TV show looking for a spouse. There are also very few wrong ones. Mostly, there are just reasons, and as with the contingencies that enable us to do most things, they're neither good nor bad — they're just descriptive. They're just there.

And besides, if one really is looking for heterosexual romantic life partnership, I'm not convinced that *The Bachelor* is such a bad way to go about it. Dovetailing with its increased reflection of the world we live in, the show has really turned around its batting average on successful coupling. And while it's true that the show has a pretty terrible track record for converting engagements to marriages, it's also true that no *Bachelor* marriage has ended in divorce, and every married couple now has children. A generation of *Bachelor* spawn. Not that procreating means happily ever after or whatever, but my point is that the unions yielded by *The Bachelor* seem just like all marriages: arrangements that answer to a complicated knot of social, economic, and biological needs and desires. There are no right reasons — but there are plenty of right conditions.

There's something I want to be clear about from the beginning of our own journey: I fucking love *The Bachelor*. I may be a critic, but I'm also a fan. Consider me a regular at the feelings trough. And I don't think *The Bachelor* is good at being bad, or good in spite of itself: I think it is truly great television

— compulsively entertaining, bizarrely moving, and harrowingly smart. I think if we let it, *The Bachelor* has something to teach us: something about a when and a where (today, and America), but also something that reaches further and deeper, something more basic about what it means to be human at all.

Each episode of *The Bachelor* culminates in a rose ceremony: a weekly rite by which the lead reveals whom he'd like to keep on the show, winnowing down the dating pool until there is just the one who was right there in front of him all along. For this ceremonial dumping (or romancing, depending on which side of it you're on), contestants gather in rows while the Bachelor calls forth the names of those he's chosen, asking each one whether she will "accept this rose" as a token of his continued interest.

It wasn't always going to be roses. Or there's some debate about it, anyway; in an oral history for *The Cut* in 2016, Chris Harrison recalls that the production team considered other trinkets and tokens as a way of visualizing the week's winners. But in Mike Fleiss's memory, things are clearer. As he remembers it, he was always sure: the rose was the rose was the rose.

Now it seems impossible that it could have been anything else, like *The Bachelor* might have flopped had they chosen garlands or promise rings or pearls. The rose is the perfect *Bachelor* item, the ultimate symbol of romantic love as both destiny and choice. Consider Juliet on her balcony, already crossed by the stars, talking to herself about knowing the difference between what you feel and what you've been taught. The rose reminds you to trust your instincts.

And those *Bachelor* roses are specimens. Thorn-free stems long and straight as magic wands, each one capped by the kind of deep, decadent bloom that appears at the very end of a growing season, right before everything turns to rot and dies. They're not natural, of course: they're plastic, or fabric, or some state-of-the-art material by which only the very best artificial flowers are made. Maybe they smell like some chemical, abusive manufacturing process, or maybe they're laced with perfume. They might smell like static, like dust. Nothing at all. But they're clearly roses — what else would you call them?

Of course love is real. That doesn't mean it isn't also fake.

1

One-on-One Time: Romance

Time bends on *The Bachelor*. For one thing, its passage is parsed in weeks, as if love's progress was some form of gestation hitting developmental milestones, scaling up from lima bean to lemon to dragon fruit. And within this episodic unfurling, contestants suffer the effects of time turned lopsided. *Bachelor* time is like chewing gum: it can be plied (between producers' fingers) into something stringy, attenuated, stuck on itself one moment, the next squashed into an indigestible rubber pebble that will haunt your colon for seven years.

For long stretches of filming, every hour is an off-hour. Denied anything to watch or click or scroll or read, contestants kill time in the *Bachelor* mansion with what remains to them: eating, drinking, and saying more than they mean to. In contrast with this surfeit of leisure time, minutes spent in the direct presence of the show's lead are scarce. Referred to as "one-on-one time" — sometimes even shortened to just "time" because everyone knows what kind matters — contestants arrive on set hungry for it and stay never quite sated. It's the one resource every contestant, no matter what other advantages they might possess, needs in order to conceive and develop romance. As one contestant puts it: "Time is the most important thing in this entire process. You don't get time — you're going home. Because how is any relationship going to form if you don't have time?" Time is also the one thing guaranteed to remain in higher demand than supply: until the show's final minutes, there are necessarily more suitors than there are objects of affection.

The way the Bachelor's[2] time is doled out among contestants is, like all things on the show, highly controlled. This begins episode one, with the opening night cocktail party and rose ceremony. Picture prom crossed with dodgeball picks crossed with pulling an all-nighter (the sun can often be seen rising as the first rejects hobble away from the mansion in tears that seem as likely to be the result of drunk exhaustion as hurt feelings). During this marathon of first encounters, the only time each woman is guaranteed to spend alone with the Bachelor is her "limo exit": a quick meet-and-greet in the driveway of the *Bachelor* mansion, closer to the length of a TV commercial than a theatrical trailer. Contestants take a range of approaches — from awkward to gimmicky to casual

---

2 Here and elsewhere, I use *The Bachelor* as a default because it came first. It's usually more or less a straight gender-swap for *The Bachelorette*, though there are aspects of the latter (mostly surrounding proposals) where the vise grip of gender roles prevents a one-to-one translation.

to sincere — to make this short moment their own, trying to fix themselves in the lead's memory (remember, he's going through at least 25 of these in a row).

Regardless of what they do to distinguish themselves (or not), practically every limo exit ends with the promise to "see you inside."[3] But on the inside there are no guarantees: it's a free-for-all on the Bachelor's time, and once the parade of limos has delivered the show's full cast, the mansion turns Darwinian. What ensues is something like the full-contact version of speed-dating: as roller derby is to gliding in circles under the spangled watch of a disco ball. The only rule of cocktail party engagement is that when a contestant asks if she might "steal" him, the Bachelor and his interlocutor must comply. This rule is never explicitly stated, but it becomes clear if you're a regular viewer that contestants have been armed with this passive-aggressive code word in order to facilitate the lead's frequent changing of hands (and stoke resentment between contestants). The night (which at this point has become the next day) ends in the first rose ceremony. The first *Bachelor* cut is the deepest, with 10 to 12 participants axed from the original cull of 25 or more.

Those who make the team move into the mansion, and now the production of romance is really underway. Each week, cards arrive to invite contestants out on dates in various for-mations: one-on-one, or in packs up to a dozen strong.[4] Time

---

3 It's hard to know whether contestants are instructed to deliver this line or whether, like other bobbles of *Bachelor*ese, this is a cue they've internalized.

4 At least once per season, there is also a "two-on-one" date that forces the Bachelor's hand in choosing between two women.

alone with the Bachelor in the form of a one-on-one is the most coveted, but also the highest risk. The date comes with a rose the Bachelor might deliver to secure the contestant's place on the show for another week and spare her sweating through ceremonial picks at the end of the episode; not getting the rose, however, means instant elimination. Back at the mansion, a black-clad tech will arrive to signal the rejected woman's departure by silently carting her suitcase away.

For many weeks, though, the majority of dates happen in groups. These are divided into two parts: a daytime activity followed by an evening cocktail party in miniature. The latter half of the group date includes a rose, which the lead will use to single out a contestant and bestow on her another week's worth of insurance.

On group dates, the first half of the date is generally devoted to some participatory, comfort-zone-breaching activity. From Muay Thai to stand-up comedy to Turkish oil wrestling to burlesque to teaching sex ed to kids, these dates more closely resemble the zany group bonding activities of some middle-management leadership retreat than they do everyday romance. While all group dates are implicitly competitions for time, attention, and the security of a rose, when the activity is something that can be measurably won or lost, that competition is often literalized, with only the winners continuing on to "get more time" on the second, rose-inclusive half of the date. "This volleyball game is the most important game of my life," one *Bachelor* contestant (who is about to lose the most important game of her life) notes, adding, "You're talking about more time with a guy who could potentially be yours forever. This is that big a deal."

The last chance for "time" each week comes in the form of a final cocktail party before each rose ceremony, a last-ditch shot for contestants to corner the lead one-on-one and make a case for their marital suitability. This cocktail party is occasionally canceled when the lead's mind is made up and they would prefer (understandably) not to suffer the hassling-slash-courtship of desperate people they're on the brink of rejecting.

The way the show moulds time — giving contestants too much of one kind and not enough of another — is the backbone of *The Bachelor* and *Bachelorette*. Warped time forms the underlying structural logic of each episode. It is both the carrot and the stick by which contestants are moved to competition — pumped up to crave the time they get, needled into acting out in its absence.

So, now you know how *Bachelor*-time is bundled into a game show format, but you might be wondering, *Where does romance come into all this?* Here we turn to content as well as form: what happens in that one-on-one time is as important as the ways in which it is doled out. Provoked by some combination of producer pressure, knowledge of the show's mores, and the genuine urgency of a short production schedule,[5] Bachelor

---

5 It will probably not surprise you to know that weekly episodes and weeks of real-time filming do not line up. Depending on the season, filming appears to take place over around eight to ten weeks.

couples develop feelings in ways that are so targeted and so effective, it feels more accurate to say they are engineered than that they grow.

The primary tool used to make love happen is something so basic it seems almost too elemental to be as next-level efficient as it is: good old-fashioned storytelling. (Well, sort of old-fashioned, and sort of good.) Contestants do not slowly reveal themselves with facts, anecdotes, and opinions in the usual way of workaday daters. The show's time constraints require that acts of self-revelation be both more potent and more ritualized. Thus *Bachelor* contestants don't talk about themselves; they (prematurely, inorganically) "share their story."

"The things that I'm going to tell her today — these are things that she has to know," one contestant says. "I need to open up," says another. On a one-on-one date, Bachelorette Andi Dorfman notes about one of her suitors, "He has this huge story that — I feel it weighing [him] down. Like, I can sit across from [him] and know that he just wants to burst out with this story and tell me who he is."

Confessional narrative is a form of *Bachelor* currency. When contestants fear they are at risk of becoming a missed connection and/or being sent home, they use brief windows of one-on-one time to spill whatever has been designated (likely in conjunction with producers) their beans. Having and telling a story lights up brief one-on-one moments with bright, unmissable emotional charge.

The result is that the show has a really interesting (some might say exploitative) relationship to trauma. Because when contestants go searching for a personal mythology, what they come up with tends to be pretty much the worst shit that's ever happened to them.

The ostensible idea here is not that the contestant is looking for pity, but that they are providing evidence of themselves. And the show insists on this distinction. Take, for example, Andi's one-on-one date with suitor Dylan. Dylan's story is a doozy: dad ditched the family early, and in the last few years both his siblings have died of drug overdoses, the most recent just a few months before filming (hey, just throwing this out there: maybe not such a great moment to launch your reality TV career). To cap it off, they're on a steam train rolling through the part of New England where Dylan grew up, passing sites of childhood memories.

DYLAN: I don't want you to feel bad for me.

ANDI: I do feel bad. I *should* feel bad.

DYLAN: But I don't want you to just keep me around because of that. Please don't. I am who I am because of what's happened in my life. And I've grown so much because of it, I really have . . . I want somebody who I can tell these things to and [who] will respect me for me, and not my family or what I've been through . . . I just told you everything that's happened to me in the last four years of my life, which is more than most of my friends know.

The contestant uses their story to sketch the contours of their character, and the lead confirms the value of those character traits with the offer of a continuing role in the show's narrative. On a one-on-one date, it's generally a very brief trip from confessional to rose. "I have never in my life been so moved," Andi tells Dylan. "The fact that you are sitting here and willing to tell me, willing to be raw and open and say those things. I just feel like we're open, and this is the start. With that being said, will you accept this rose?"

On her *Bachelorette* season, Desiree (Des) Hartsock was especially prone to hustle to the conclusion that her pursuers' traumas were evidence of something "positive." "Brandon's such a positive energy," she says of one mega sad sack who has just incontinently spilled a lifetime's worth of neglect in a manner so attention-starved it seems likely no woman had ever made direct eye contact with him before. Their conversation is like a therapy session with erotic transference, not so much a first date (it's actually not even a date — he's just cornered her at a cocktail party). Though Des doesn't keep Brandon around long after this incident, she refuses to admit that he's a total bummer. "I saw such kindness in his heart when he's telling the story about his childhood," she persists.

In other instances, Des is so desperate to get to the good part that she starts writing the contestant's story for him. "What makes Drew Drew?" she asks on a one-on-one shortly before hometowns. Drew goes on to describe his father, who is a recovering alcoholic, crying as he tells Des a story from his childhood:

DREW: Actually it's the first time I've said that.

DES: Really? This whole time?

DREW: Yeah, ever. [*he cries, she hugs him*] Um . . . yeah I certainly haven't told anybody what that conversation was like. Anyway, so he's sober. And he's a huge part of the AA community.

DES: [*interrupting*] Helping other people . . . You just gave me goosebumps. Because I think that's great that he can turn it into something so positive.

But wait, there's more to Drew's sad tale! Dad isn't just in recovery; he's also sick.

DREW: My father tells me that he has cancer . . . he took something that could have just wrecked your world and it almost amplified what the meaning was . . . There's so much strength. I really don't think many people know that he has cancer.

DES: [*interrupting*] He's just so positive.

Des's interruptions are telling: she wants to get to the part with the meaning and the good feelings. And in *Bachelor* logic, she is not wrong to be preemptive. She knows where this is going: Drew is a great guy because he's been through a lot.

"You've got to know, though, you are a great person to know," she tells him. "Thank you for sharing that. It gives me a glimpse into who you are." In an interview with producers, she confirms that she "really enjoyed hearing his story about his dad."

I'll pause here for a moment to say: there's something about the actual content of contestants' tragic stories that feels important to mention. Something that speaks to how and for whom this show is relevant. It's hard to place — just a feeling you start to get when, say, you marathon through dozens of episodes of *The Bachelor* and *Bachelorette* in a row. Watch each season's love object cornered over and over, subjected to a seemingly endless volley of punishing, neatly packaged revelations, and it's hard to shake the thought *This is all so American.*

The shit that has happened to these people is at once idiosyncratic and archetypal. These are born-in-the-USA highs and lows. A potpourri of *Bachelor* and *Bachelorette* stories: A flunked-out pro baseball player competes with his NFL-drafted sibling for parental love. A stepfather shoots his wife with a sawed-off shotgun in front of her kids (I could not make this up if I wanted to). Absentee fathers, struggling single moms, addicted siblings. Someone has an eating disorder. Someone else has diabetes. There is death by overdose, death by cardiac arrest, death by private plane. In recent seasons, veterans of America's wars in Afghanistan and Iraq have been tapped as a resource of the kind of people the show loves best: traumatized ones with hot bods.

These are stories that could only come out of a place defined by having both too much and too little, from a population bisected into the one and the ninety-nine. The bad things that happen in a country packed with the equal-opportunity vices of the affluent and the poor: guns, cars, drugs. The bad things that happen in country at war with itself and just actually at war. The bad things that happen to lovers and defenders of "freedom."

Just as telling are the absent narratives. Never once have I seen a contestant tell a story about sexual assault.[6] There are few examples of immigrant families, language barriers, racial discrimination. *The Bachelor*'s trauma roundup is weirdly selective, inconsistently sanitized. This is white America.[7]

It's not only the content that feels willfully and limitedly American — it's also an ethos betrayed by the way the stories are framed. Take, for example, this confession issued by Catherine Giudici on a one-on-one date during Sean Lowe's 2013 season of *The Bachelor*:

> One thing that's been really important to me and that's helped me shaped my life is a very traumatic experience at 12 . . . My best friend and I went to summer camp . . . about a hundred feet into this trail we hear this crack. It's a tree falling, and it fell on the girl in front of me

---

6 Only the right kind of trauma is wanted on this journey: a form of violence experienced by nearly one in five American women (according to the Centers for Disease Control and Prevention) need not apply.

7 More on the show's blinding whiteness in Chapter 7.

and killed her instantly. And at 12 years old, I realized that things can be taken from you very quickly. And I learned very, very early that my biggest goal in life was to be in love, and have a family, and have a partner for life. So that's why I'm here: because I knew going into this that you wanted that too. That's why I want to be with you — because I know that we could be great.

Again and again, using similar language, contestants transform trauma into fated, faithful resilience. They say what they've been through has made them who they are today. They say it made them realize what's important (no matter how unrelated the event, these values are squarely on *Bachelor* brand: romance, family, the desire to procreate). It made them realize life is short. It made them.

Bachelor-believers allow that contestants must fess up to their personal tragedies, and we forgive the often shoehorned nature of those confessions. We do so because the stories are compelling and we are thirsty voyeurs, and because the urgency of the show's compressed time frame is contagious. Having made these concessions to *Bachelor* logic, however, both contestants and viewers are quick to outrage when they sense that someone is exaggerating, leaning on, or otherwise exploiting their "story" to gain the lead's attention.

Successful *Bachelor* and *Bachelorette* contestants tell stories that deliver a clean, uncomplicated arc, but they appear to arrive at a conclusion through innocent, almost blithe intro-spection. There is a hierarchy being sketched here: contestants are rewarded for being self-aware, but skewered for being self-conscious. Stories — of traumas overcome, lessons learned, characters formed — must be tidy but unpolished. The con-testant must deliver a strong sense of who they are without seeming too aware of how they come across. This line between heartfelt and manipulative is a delicate but powerful tripwire. Crossing it is not only a question of succeeding on *The Bachelor*; it often means the difference between being cast as one season's villain and being tapped for the next season's romantic lead.[8]

The high quotient of sob stories on the show is something contestants are well aware of. As one woman surveying the playing field on her season says, "Every girl here is amazing. Everyone has a story too. So it's like I'm not the only one who has been through something." Another is both more pointed and more astute as she grouses tearfully about a competitor's edge: "Because she has a story that is so much more trauma-tizing than [mine], she got to go talk to him and I couldn't. My story is just, like, obviously nothing compared to hers, and now it's a big comparison game of sad stories." Ding ding ding! This is, indeed, an accurate description of the first level of *The Bachelor* as game show. Round one: sad story show-down. A tragic tale will not secure you the win, but it may keep you in the game long enough to get more time, cultivate a connection, and level up.

---

8 More on this in Chapter 3 on Villains.

Of course, sharing the deeply held narratives that define your values, your beliefs, your very self: that's a real part of falling in real love. What's weird isn't that this happens on *The Bachelor* — it's that this intimate act is somehow *not* voided by the brutally public, inorganic conditions under which it occurs. Because in real life, confessional storytelling is alchemized into romantic love via the catalyst of privacy. Exchanging revelation for reception, vulnerability for empathy, has an only-we-two, world-building function. Confession to a beloved is a means of closing ranks, indulging in a fantasy of the greater world's irrelevance, turning personal privacy into something built for two. It's zipping your sleeping bags together, ducking under the covers, whispering into the dark.

On *The Bachelor*, we are privy to confessions made under circus-grade floodlights — intimate moments quite literally produced by professionals for broadcast to millions. What's remarkable is that even in this apparent total absence of privacy, the show still somehow manages to spin contestants' raw trauma into romantic gold.

Hot tip: if you are ever cast on *The Bachelor* or *Bachelorette*, do not admit your phobias to anyone you meet. Even better, fake a terror of something you've always wanted to do but lacked the opportunity or means. Because if producers know you are possessed of some fear, you can count on being forced to face it in some lavish, hyperbolic way for the benefit of the person you are trying to date (not to mention the rest of America).

The show's relationship to trauma is not just about stories told: date activities themselves are often lightly — or not-so-lightly — traumatic. Group dates put contestants on display in uncomfortable ways, but one-on-one dates can be downright *Fear Factor*–esque. Bachelor couples shuffle over traffic-chocked bridges on cables, are locked in horror-themed escape rooms, free-fall off cliffs, rappel the glass façades of buildings swayed by icy winds, dangle into holes that look like they reach the center of the earth. *The Bachelor* would have you believe no one could ever fall in love without belaying there.

These extreme dates bond couples through experiences that are not merely scary, but designed to activate a bodily sense of mortal danger. Even non-terror-oriented date itineraries tend less towards balmy pleasure and more towards perception-shattering surreality. Couples might be cradled in the webbed palm of a catamaran and whipped over turquoise water, dropped like sexy survivalists on an uninhabited island of talcum sand. This is pleasure in extremis, dating in Technicolor. Experiences that vibrate beyond the standard register of emotional pitch. On *The Bachelor*, good times will flood and overwhelm, not comfort.

Here's the thing. For all its reliance on fantasy and tapping the human capacity for imagination, *The Bachelor* is also brought to you by science. This is romance as neurology, love as a chemical equation: adrenaline plus dopamine over limited time. With no room in the production schedule to guarantee couples will fall in love, they are flung, dangled, and tossed there.

"If we can do this, we can do anything. Leap of faith," says Kiptyn on Jillian's season of *The Bachelorette* as they navigate a ropes course. "I think that's exactly how falling in love is: you're sitting on the edge, you're scared, and you just have to let go and do it," says Molly on Jason's season about a tandem bungee jump. In addition to being a wellspring of easy metaphors for love, this strategy also just *works*.[9] On *The Bachelor*, watch it happen before your very eyes: two people bumble through first-date-jittery small talk as they are delivered to the top of a building, and by the time they've free-fallen to the bottom, there's chemistry.

When not being rattled into love, *Bachelor* couples talk. The show's use of "story" is not restricted to contestants' well-packaged personal histories. *The Bachelor* works narrative from the micro to the macro, nesting stories within one another like matryoshka dolls. Zooming out, the season as a whole is a quest narrative: the lead's journey to find love. Along the way, every time the lead is paired off with any one contestant, they spend a good portion of their time telling one another the story of the relationship they are, in that very second, in the process of building.

The story being told is self-reflexive, the characters and

---

9 A now-classic psychological study from the University of British Columbia in the 1970s tested for "misattribution of arousal" by seeing whether male subjects were more likely to phone a woman if they meet her immediately after crossing a scarily rickety suspension bridge. (Spoiler: they were.) Later studies have used roller coasters and even just regular physical exertion to similarly demonstrate that riling the nervous system primes us for romance.

their relationship to one another made in the moment they say it. This concurrence of speech and action is, in fact, a crucial technique of the show's production. "In the Moment" interviews (ITMs) occur when cast members are pulled aside during filming and cajoled into delivering a present-tense description of the experience they're in the midst of having.[10] ITM footage is used to narrate the show through both documentary-style talking heads and voice-over. This creates dramatic irony for the viewer, indulging us in the illusion that we have access to characters' inner monologues. It allows us to better parse their behavior for signs that they are lying either to us, to their dates, or to themselves.

The ITMs make for an interesting trade-off: the actual experiences being documented and lived through are interrupted and stalled (again, staggering and warping participants' experience of lived time) in the service of making the story of those experiences smoother. I submit that this is not only for viewers' sakes. While ITMs are clearly fodder for the editing room and a big part of engineering storylines after the fact, I can't help but think that giving these interviews works a story-making magic on participants too. The ITM narrows the gap between experience and reflection, blending *living through* something with *talking through* it.

And as anyone who's ever written in a diary, or sent an emo email, or talked out a problem with their friends (so, like, everyone) knows, putting language to experience is not just

---

10 This is not unique to *The Bachelor* — it's a staple of unscripted TV.

reflective — it's quite literally creative. Naming a thing makes it real. (I'm not super up on my Bible, but I'm pretty sure that's the Book of Genesis takeaway.) In the case of *The Bachelor*, being asked to label every flutter and gurgle as evidence of what you are feeling surely has a way of making those feelings — and the story they serve — come to life. In the moment.

In early episodes, contestants are driven to use "time" to tell their story. As the competition reduces its numbers and the desperation of the time-scramble eases, the game show levels up to a new phase: contestants must now imagine that their story and the show's story are one and the same yarn. Past a certain point, contestants must use one-on-one time not to reveal their past, but to admit to their vision of the future and confess the depth of their feelings to the lead in spite of an inevitable absence of reassurance.[11] Basically there's a point in every season — usually at around three or four suitors left standing — when it takes an L-bomb to earn a rose.[12]

Contestants on the show are both the characters that populate the love story and its co-authors. The show empowers-slash-coerces them to narrate their stories, and then uses the

---

11 It's a half-stated rule of the game (and likely a contractual obligation) that the lead not deliver verbal confirmation of love until the final episode. That said, there have been slip-ups, most infamously from Ben Higgins, who said those three little words to *both* of his final two. My theory on this: a little starry-eyed and buzzed, he let it slip to one by accident, and then was given a nudge from production to even the playing field with the other.

12 Although there's a point at which an "I love you" becomes unofficially mandatory, professions of love can also backfire, cueing the lead to recognize a lack of reciprocal feeling and end the relationship there. It's possibly the most humiliating thing that can happen to a *Bachelor* or *Bachelorette* contestant. And it happens a lot.

material they provide to tell *The Bachelor*'s story: a singular journey that feeds on the power of the casualties it leaves behind. Again building narratives within narratives, the show stirs up multiple romantic eddies only to let them spin out and fail, swallowed in the whirlpool of an ex-post-facto–fated love. Contestants risk that the story they've signed on to both live through and tell — their tumble into romance, the building and breaking of their feelings — is destined to be pencil-scratched in the margins, an erasable gloss on someone else's marriage plot.

Participants who exercise any form of self-protection against the reasonable possibility that theirs will not prove to be the central storyline are seen as victims of "thinking too much" and "putting up walls." Even practical, functional walls — like, say, levees, or load-bearing ones — are considered deadly romance-blockers on *The Bachelor*. Contestants are expected to strip down, disarm, and give themselves over to a tidal wave of fate they are statistically more likely to wind up the victim of than the lone survivor.

Way back in 2002, the inaugural Bachelor Alex Michel — an almost mythological franchise figure who has long been off the *Bachelor* grid — precisely articulated the conundrum late-season couples face. Attempting to scale the reasonable but not exactly TV-friendly barriers put up by one of his final three (forget the fantasy suite: she wouldn't even wear a one-piece in front of him), Alex surmises, "She can't give herself to me emotionally until I know that she's the one, and I can't decide that she's the one until she gives herself to me emotionally." And so it was forever after, for seasons and seasons to come, amen.

So, here's the thing: just because romance is produced in unreal conditions, doesn't mean it isn't real. Because no matter how controlled, artificial, or even straight-up inauthentic the modes of its production may seem (or actually be), romantic love cannot exist — is simply not viable — outside the human mind, human body, human experience. That it is tethered to consciousness — to *subjectivity* — makes love impossible to ever fully objectify. Romantic feeling may be misguided, mis-understood, and misplaced, but it can never truly be made into a product, and in this, it is quietly, inexorably resistant to the machinery of capital. I'm saying the cliché is true, but it only tells you something useful when you flip the perspective: you can sell a love story, but you can't sell actual love.

Besides, if we take at face value *The Bachelor*'s aim to foster not only love, but hetero matrimony, who's to say the condi-tions the show provides are really so inauthentic? Who's to say parades of stories and flirtations with trauma aren't pretty legit ways to prepare for a marriage? After all, a big part of being with someone forever is getting down with all their stories: signing off on the ones past, agreeing to co-inhabit protagonism ever after into the future. And what is growing old together — your bodies decaying and meandering towards death — if not shared trauma? It just happens really slowly. It just takes a really long time.

2

Please Use This Key: Sex

Here's a math problem crossed with a riddle: if one man is dating 25 women, and he has 30 dates to go on in eight weeks, and he takes anywhere between one and twelve women with him on each date, then what's a three-date rule? *The Bachelor*'s answer: you can have sex as soon as you're only dating three women at once.

It's not enough to trot out the everymen and everywomen and prod at their fears of winding up alone — for a show about non-famous randos going on dates to be even a little bit watchable, it has to deliver some sexy. If all we wanted from *The Bachelor* was its relatable romantic normalcy, we might as well spend that Monday night primetime spot at Starbucks watching any couple of white people[13] break down their OkCupid match percentage. *The Bachelor* needs fantasy. And that fantasy needs sex.

The Bachelor casts human beings who embody a particular kind of standard-issue fuckability: a consistent, if indistinct, hotness. This is most striking in the first episode of each season, when the full assembly of similar-looking men or women emerge from limousine-cocoons to colonize the *Bachelor* mansion. Call it a plenty-of-fish effect: a combination of homogeneity and volume that tickles whatever dark, primordial corner of the brain thrills to the presence of an abundant resource. Without any one person needing to be especially good-looking, the first night's cocktail party seems like a room full of beautiful people.

And *The Bachelor* and *Bachelorette* catchment does turn up examples of stunning physical beauty — men and women primed for the passport to n-level celebrity they're all but guaranteed to be issued if they stay on the show long enough. More than necessarily *being* attractive, though, what contestants have in common are looks that display knowledge of what is *considered* attractive. The common denominator among the men and women who appear on the show each season is that they present as people who know what mainstream beauty standards are and have made personal choices aimed at meeting those standards. It's an aesthetic that references sexual attraction without necessarily or specifically embodying it, resulting in a dominant

---

13 It me! I'm definitely a white person, and though I've never gone on a date to Starbucks, all of my underwear is from the Gap.

look that's less a set of features and more an effect: a pixelated, approximate sexiness — the sense that everything is in the right place. There are whole seasons you could watch at a squint and not notice the difference.

Between the love object and their suitors there needs to be enough sexual interest on display to titillate the audience, but it can't be so overwhelming or ungoverned that its reach across multiple relationships registers as sleaze. The show has to achieve a very particular balance: serving up a fantasy of plenitude, variety of experience, and choice, but preserving the possibility for the spread to include a love that is peerless, fated, *un*chosen. The show must exude an aura of sexual charge without degrading the audience's ability to believe a singular, marriage-bound romance will be raised from out of the phero-mone frenzy. All this is to say: *The Bachelor* must imply limitless sexual potential, but carefully control actual sex.

And *Bachelor* couples *do* have sex — or at least the opportu-nity for it. The opening for couples to sleep together arrives in the third-to-last episode: when only three contestants remain, each is invited to spend an overnight date alone with their beloved in a "fantasy suite."

In order to understand how this goes down, it's impor-tant to know where the fantasy suites are placed in the con-text of the season. There have occasionally been tweaks to this order of operations (and larger deviations we'll get to later), but in its classical form, the overnight dates are sandwiched between hometown visits and a final proposal. On the home-town dates, the Bachelor travels across America meeting four clans of would-be in-laws, absurdly asking parents (if possible fathers, because patriarchy) for the blessing to propose to each woman, just in case. Remember, he hasn't even slept with any of these women yet. Just let that sink in for a second: sex is conceived here as a junction *between* talking to someone's family about marriage and talking to the person you're actually going to marry.

After hometowns, the Bachelor bumps off one contestant (common reasons include: he doesn't really know her, or the family skeeved him out) and moves on with his final three to a foreign destination that is often, though not always, equatorial (distracting collisions of dresswear, grooming, and humidity ensue).

Now the sex-op. Successive dinner dates with each woman come with a card tucked stealthily under a napkin or into the Bachelor's jacket. "Should you choose to forego your individual rooms," the missive addressed to both parties and signed by host Chris Harrison reads, "please use this key to stay as a couple in the fantasy suite."

Though Harrison does not specify, contestants and viewers know that the overnight dates aren't just a nudge to go at it. They also offer (as contestants frequently overstate when accepting the invitation) a precious opportunity to be truly alone. Fantasy suites come with no cameras, no mics: it's the only off-the-record time the couple is allowed during approximately two months of taping. (Cameras actually do track the pair into the suite, but only long enough to collect footage of the couple making out in a hot tub or tumbling onto a petal-strewn bed, a bedroom door swinging shut, a window shot from the outside as a light finally, suggestively goes out.)

The fantasy suite invitation has remained the same since season one. Contestants and audiences know the card is coming, and they know down to the word what it will say. But statements of the obvious are the bread and butter of *Bachelor* conventions, and so the ritual includes the lead telling the date that they "have something for them," and asking them to "read it and tell me what you think." This is not a read-in-your-head like a normal person thing: the date has to actually recite the invitation aloud. At three sentences and around 40 words,[14] the note is just long enough to generate a portrait of the romantic as a middle-schooler hooked on phonics. But it's not only the (sometimes worrisome) snapshot of basic literacy that makes this moment a beautifully crafted specimen of awkward: the reading kicks off a back-and-forth that is almost unavoidably burdened and formal. The conversations that ensue from a fantasy suite invitation are usually pretty representative not only of that particular relationship, but of any given season's tenor overall: the more controlled and caveat-laden the acceptance of the key, the more likely the season is to have been a dud.

Snoozer couples will take turns plunking down truisms about taking "time to talk" or "getting away from any distractions." (I especially love when they use "any" here, as though

---

14 Depending on the location Harrison welcomes them to and how descriptive he (or rather the production lackey who's been given the task of writing the note) gets. There are a lot of "beautiful island of [*blank*]"s.

the dense squad of humans laboring to make a television show around them are some gnatty, nondescript circumstance.) These programmed dialogues tend to start by front-loading the acceptance with an affirmation of some motivation that is anything other than sex.

Take, for example, Jake Pavelka's runner-up Tenley Molzahn's answer to the fantasy suite invite: "I want every second that I can have with you, so I would love to stay with you tonight." To which Jake affirms, "I absolutely cannot wait to watch our first sunrise." Similarly, Vienna Girardi, the woman to whom Jake eventually proposes, finishes reading her invitation and asks in the same breath whether Jake is a "good cuddler." "I think I'm a great cuddler," Jake tells her earnestly, and the couple agrees that they "need some time." And that's how, without watching another minute of this season, you know Jake sucks.

Here's a question I can't work out an answer to: when couples do these bits, do even *they* know what part of the performance is for one another and what is for the audience? I can't tell — and I can't tell if *they* can tell — whether these declarations are intended to mask suggestion with innocence or innocence with suggestion. Is the innuendo really as obvious as it seems? Is vocalizing a plan to not fuck the most flirtatious way this couple has in their repertoire to agree to fuck? And/or are these statements more like just-for-the-record insurance clauses aimed to put them beyond the reproach of a conservative audience they feel beholden to? Are these lines for the benefit of daddy-daughter-dance-type parents? Who is saving face from whom? And is it at all possible that these conversations really *are* about putting limits on physical intimacy? Is there some schematic of references I'm missing? (Is a "sunrise" a BJ?)

There are, of course, many examples of couples who don't bother with any of this: dates who practically leap from the table yelling "Yeehaw!" Those can be just as awkward and stilted as the conservative "let's just talk all night"-ers. The truth is, milking humanity and natural chemistry out of the fantasy suite invitation is tough.

There are ways, though, to come off as relatively chill here. Consider single Seattle dad Jason Mesnick, whose time as Bachelor came one season before Jake's. It tells you something about Jason's season to know that on two out of his three fantasy suite dates, the women flipped the script. Jillian Harris (who you might know from her post-*Bachelor* life on *Love It or List It Vancouver*) doesn't go through the usual rigmarole of playing cute over the card's arrival, but asks Jason directly, "Do you have something to give me tonight?" Jason is thrown off-book, pretty much asking Jill for his next line: "Do I have something to give you? You're asking *me* now?" He hands her the card, and in answer to the customary "What do you think?" Jill zags again, turning the line of questioning back on Jason: "Do you think you can handle a whole night with me?" His next date, Molly Malaney (now Molly Mesnick), goes a step further, preempting Harrison's letter with a homemade alt-fantasy-suite card of her own inviting Jason to spend the night with her. Conclusion: good season.

Then there are Bachelors and Bachelorettes who skip the fantasy suite altogether. Emily Maynard — a soft-drawling single mom who could serve as the prototype for Southern Belle Barbie — opts out to "set an example" for her young daughter. On her would-be-overnight with the man who would become her final pick, one-f Jef Holm, she offers him the invitation apparently only to test his commitment to killing buzz. He acts like "a gentleman" and declines. The couple uses the fantasy suite to stage a chaste, pre-bed chat until Jef declares it "time for us to bridle these passions" and heads to his own room. Nothing like a good bridling, I always say. See the cool thing about Jef is that he was obviously a time-traveler visiting us from a more-animal-husbandry-literate past. And he didn't restrict himself to anachronisms from his own epoch, either, but brought gifts from the full breadth of his temporal journeys, performing his limo exit on a skateboard and flipping it into the bushes with what can only be described as '90s spunk. (Alright, jk, Jef Holm wasn't from another time — he was just Mormon. He and Maynard broke off their engagement after a few months.)

With the fantasy suites, *The Bachelor* acknowledges the necessary relationship between sexual intimacy and lasting romance while also putting hard-and-fast constraints on its expression. It's a ritual characterized by typical *Bachelor*-esque extremes: the long stretch of celibacy followed by the quick catapult to successive one-nighters with multiple, often highly emotionally invested partners (or at least highly brainwashed ones, which is, in one way, the ultimate form of investment) just a few days before presumably committing to one of them for life. Held up to most real-world norms, this is absurd. It's not any one element that is unimaginable; it's the sum of the parts — the proximity of the all to the nothing. Like all things *Bachelor*, the fantasy suites manage to be at once too much and not enough.

The fantasy suite might be the most concentrated example of *Bachelor* logic and its powerful reversals. Because the suite's appeal is not the kitted out hotel or the vacation setting: it's the opportunity to press pause on all the fantasy-making machinery. The show has successfully turned normalcy into a fantasy. The mystery around what will go down between these couples under normalized conditions is a major part of *Bachelor* lore, a critical junction in the arc of the hero's journey. Anticipation of the fantasy suites cranks up slowly over many episodes, and their aftermath suffuses everything that follows. The rose ceremony following the overnights is especially burdened with the unfortunate implication that it's a referendum on an individual's goods in the sack.

The fantasy suite episode also changes the viewer's position. Until now, a good portion of the show's narrative tension is generated through our enjoyment of dramatic irony. Between witnessing group dynamics, dates, and In the Moment interviews, we see — or are encouraged by the show's editors to believe we see — the romantic playing field from a greater vantage than any of its players. The overnight dates unseat our reign as know-it-alls, returning some narrative power to the men and women who have been performing their lived experience for our pleasure. Fantasy suites are a lacuna, a blind spot in the audience's surveillance. As one contestant puts it: "It's like Vegas: what happens in the fantasy suite stays in the fantasy suite."

The urgent feeling that we have been left out of something generates enough suspense to carry us through the last two episodes: a storyline-stalling "Men/Women Tell All" reunion/recap, and on to the final choice and possible proposal. But the show's ending does not always resolve the tension the fantasy suites have generated offscreen. The content of those few dark hours can be spun into years' worth of *Bachelor* paraphernalia: glossy interviews, book deals, perennial cryptic tweets.

These hints and admissions are strictly relegated to the show's margins. On Andi Dorfman's season of *The Bachelorette*, runner-up Nick Viall violated this code by taking the opportunity presented on "After the Final Rose" to stutter at the Bachelorette: "Knowing how in love with you I was, if you weren't in love with me, I'm just not sure why, why you made love with me?" Andi shuts this down as "below the belt" and "something that should be private." Nick is immediately shunted to the Bachelor Nation shit list.[15]

One criticism of *The Bachelor* and *Bachelorette* is that these shows, and by extension the people who appear on them, are

---

15 Nick's subsequent franchise appearances would prove this hatred to be impermanent, and he would go on to become the Bachelor himself. We'll talk more about Viall's tumble and rehabilitation through the *Bachelor* franchise in Chapter 6.

superficial. I would argue, though, that the fantasy suite ritual offers just one example of the way the show in fact demands highly evolved emotional, intellectual, and (probably in some cases) physical flexibility of participants. The fantasy suites are a total mindfuck. Emerging from such at once limited and diffuse sexual conscription to build a partnership strikes me as something that would require real imagination and empathy. It's a testament to the show's powerful logic that it successfully sells the fantasy suites as a stepping stone towards fairy tale love, but it's a testament to the people who go through it that any of them generates actual, lasting romance from it.

Though the fantasy suite dates are the only official sex hours allotted in the production schedule, *Bachelor* and *Bachelorette* contestants do allegedly find ways to discreetly bump uglies, even on the camera's watch. (Some seasons have hewn more convincingly to that fantasy of meaningful romance than others.) One time-honored method among *Bachelor* contestants looking for a quickie is to head into the sanctioned mic-free, clothing-optional zone of the ocean (an advantage of the show's many exotic locales: couples are often within frolicking distance of an ocean).

On his season of *The Bachelor*, Ben Flajnik and eventual winner Courtney Robertson took a mid-season skinny dip during which, Robertson later revealed in her tell-all *I Didn't Come Here to Make Friends*, they did have sex on camera. But "only for about 20 seconds" and, to complete the visual for you, "just the tip." (Flajnik and Robertson called off their engagement for the final time a few months after their season aired.)

Two seasons later, runner-up Clare Crawley orchestrated a similar off-hours ocean dip with Bachelor Juan Pablo Galavis (like Courtney, Clare snuck away to visit the Bachelor without other contestants' knowledge, though, unlike Courtney, she was wearing clothes). When Juan Pablo later appeared to slut-shame her for the incident, many viewers were led to believe that Juan Pablo's regrets were of the post-coital variety. Whether any *hors de* fantasy suite sex actually occurred, however, remains unconfirmed.

In earlier, simpler times, the fourth Bachelor Bob Guiney — class clown of the inaugural *Bachelorette* season, who took his run at Bachelor during a peak moment of passable-handsomeness before transmogrifying into a sweaty ball of wax — is allegedly the most laid in the show's history.[16] According to show creator Mike Fleiss, Guiney slept with "five-and-a-half women" during his season's filming. The rumor tossed up by other franchise alums is that the camera-dodging tactic was a good old-fashioned bathroom fuck. It's impossible to know if this is true: that kind of behavior might have worked on early seasons but would never escape seasoned producers attuned to drama fodder today.

---

16 At least on *The Bachelor* and *Bachelorette* proper: I might not take that bet if you threw *Bachelor Pad* and *Bachelor in Paradise* into the mix.

Let's talk virgins. *Bachelor* producers have the rare gift for persuading adults who have never had sex before to join a televised, competitive cattle-call in search of someone to have sex with for the rest of their lives. Four (known) virgins graced the show's early and middle years, and while most went home relatively early, one did make it to the final two in competition for dubiously Italian, dubiously titled prince Lorenzo Borghese on the flop of a season *The Bachelor: Rome*.

Though virgins have always dotted *The Bachelor* and *Bachelorette* landscape, the show has only relatively recently figured out how to maximize contestants' sexual inexperience as a plot point. This began with the arrival of Sean Lowe, who came third in pursuit of Emily Maynard. That Emily took a pass on her overnights was just as well for Sean, who revealed himself as a "born-again virgin" when he ascended to Bachelor. Not in the urban dictionary, haven't-been-laid-for-a-year way, but in an evangelical-frat-boy-come-to-Jesus way. Lowe says he hit the reset button on his sexual status after college, and at the time of filming the then-29-year-old had been saving (maybe more like remortgaging) himself for marriage for six years. Sean was engaged on the show to quirky designer Catherine Giudici, and the two were married on an ABC special a little over a year later.[17] In a later interview with Chris Harrison, Lowe described their long-awaited wedding night as "fireworks," which Giudici joking-not-jokingly amended to

---

17 That would make theirs the fourth televised franchise wedding, following Trista and Ryan, Jason and Molly, and Ashley and J.P.

"Quick fireworks." The couple is still married and has since welcomed their first child.

Two seasons later, Chris "Prince Farming" Soules was graced with not one but two virgins on his season of *The Bachelor*. As one shocked contestant puts it when news of the high maidenhood quotient is revealed: "We've got two virgins in the *Bachelor* mansion. Two virgins — one Chris. I can't make this up. Stay tuned."

On this season, Becca Tilley would become the second legit virgin (sorry Sean Lowe, do-overs don't count) the show has led into a fantasy suite. (She and Soules apparently did not have sex.) Though her run for Soules's affections did not last as long as Becca's, Ashley Iaconetti (dubbed "Ashley I." on the two-Ashley season) went home week six, but emerged from the season the reigning Virgin Queen of *Bachelor*land.

Ashley I. spends more energy than Becca sweating over when and how to let the untouched kitten out of the bag. She builds to it over several episodes, first revealing her predicament to Mackenzie, a 21-year-old single mom who named her toddler Kale (yes, after the vegetable) and has an anxious fascination with alien abduction. It's worth noting that in this scene both women are displaying signs of the particular kind of enthusiasm for confessional bonding that comes from being about as deep into tipsy as you can get before you're outright drunk:

ASHLEY: No, I'm a virgin. I'm like not even kidding. I am.

MACKENZIE: That's so cool.

ASHLEY: I don't know if he's going to like it or not.

MACKENZIE: No, he will like it. Every guy likes it. Because guys like taking your virginity.

ASHLEY: No, I know most guys do, except for if they're —

MACKENZIE: And Chris is going to be the kind. No seriously. I'm *jealous*. I swear to god I'm jealous that you're a virgin right now. It's going to make you stay here so much longer . . . You're super pretty, you have a good personality, and you're a virgin. Oh my God. We have to tell him.

With her appraisal that Ashley will "stay here so much longer," Mackenzie is correctly intuiting that sexual inexperience gives Ashley a story, and a story is what turns a *Bachelor* participant into a contender. This is a reminder to the virgin to make much of her (screen) time.

And so she does. Ashley's attempt to confess her lack of sin to Chris is drawn out over several episodes. In her first attempt, she wakes him from a whiskey-soggy sleep and refers obliquely to being "frickin' innocent," and a "frickin' nerd." It's several more days of agonizing over whether she's made her meaning clear to the Bachelor (she hasn't) before Ashley takes a blunter approach that does the trick (she then has a tearful meltdown over whether or not the admission went over well). In the meantime, it's only Ashley's addressing her virgin status with a larger group of women that provokes Becca Tilley to casually deadpan: "I'm a virgin too." Ashley practically spits a puff pastry on her — whether because she's thrilled to have a maiden compatriot or afraid to share her thunder is unclear — but Becca is totally unruffled: "I haven't told him. It hasn't come up."

Ashley I. would go on to star in two seasons of *Bachelor in Paradise*, logging spates of tears that seem almost supernatural in volume, but (alas? happily?) no swipes on her V-card.[18] In her most recent (though I doubt her last) franchise appearance on *Paradise* season three, Ashley's portion of the show's campy opening gambit features her dark hair draped in a holy Madonna veil as she raises her liquid-lined eyes to meet the camera. Ashley I. (who I feel the urge to note has a master's degree in journalism from a really good school) may appear to have the emotional resilience of a second-grader, but she's always game to make fun of herself, and really kind of a champ.

I bring up the virgins of *The Bachelor* not because I find the conjunction of their life choices fascinating (though I do), but because of what's revealed by the show's treatment of virginity over time. In Sean Lowe's case, his relationship to sex is explicitly a religious thing, binding his "virginity" (really celibacy)

---

18 "If you take her virginity, you will be a national treasure," Ashley's friend tells a man about to go on a date with her in *Paradise*.

up with something large swaths of Americans consider sacrosanct. The virgins offered to farmer Chris occupy a huge amount of the show's attention, and much hay is made (har-har) over revelations of virgin status. But weirdly little screen time goes towards explaining *why* either of these women is a virgin in the first place, despite the fact that, as one contestant says to Ashley I. (who agrees), "in our generation it's so not normal."

We are left with hints. Becca, for example, makes it clear that not having sex is something she's decided, not something that's happened by accident. She refers to it as "just as a choice I made" and talks explicitly about waiting for marriage. When she does eventually go into the fantasy suite with Soules (telling him only at the 11th hour that she's never had sex), she talks about "temptation." There's some implication here that this is a religious thing, but only by way of allusion. To never allow Becca to explain her choice denies her the basic, character-making function of motivation. She is flattened into a two-dimensional illustration of a cherry waiting to be popped.

Ashley I. seems to place her own virginity in the context of a broader maturity issue. "It's not anything that I'm super serious about. I'm just waiting for the right guy," she says. Every time she talks about it during this season, she mentions she's never had a boyfriend, or she is, despite her Kardashian-modeled looks, a "nerd." She is, we are left to surmise, a virgin because she is romantically inexperienced, not the other way around. Her virginity appears to be a circumstance rather than a dogmatic commitment.

The point here is that by keeping Becca's and Ashley's agency out of the frame, the show not only turns virginity into a quirky character trait, but keeps loss of virginity in the mix as a potential storyline. This is part of an overall move towards all-or-nothing narratives the show has made over time. Just as in the earliest seasons, a proposal was only a possible, producer-encouraged outcome, it has since become an expectation, and those who fail to deliver are punished by viewers. Serving up will-they-or-won't-they virgins is just another way the show raises stakes wherever it can get them. After all, this is a show that challenges each new season to be "the most dramatic." *The Bachelor* has not managed to "produce" anyone's first time . . . yet.[19] But I wouldn't put it past them.

Speaking of sex and drama and stakes, it's time to talk about my personal, all-time favorite Bachelorette: Kaitlyn Bristowe.

Some things to know about Kaitlyn: when she first entered the *Bachelor* landscape alongside Soules's virgins, Kaitlyn was a spin instructor and former dancer hailing from Leduc, Alberta, via Vancouver.[20] She is beautiful, and funny, and laughs with a crazy-lady cackle so dorky it crosses over into charming. She has a case of resting duck face she seems to come by honestly, as

19 They have managed to implicitly facilitate a sexual first for Raven Gates, who went into a Finnish fantasy suite cabin with Nick Viall saying she'd never had an orgasm, and came out prancing through the land of the midnight sun like a heroine freed from bondage in some Nordic fairy tale.

20 She appears to have since taken a post-*Bachelor* position as a successfully brand-sponsored "personality." It's a feat that, these days, many a *Bachelor* alum pulls off halfway, but few as successfully as K.B.

though she was genetically engineered to be Instagrammed. On a group date featuring a songwriting contest, when the other women serenade Chris with heartfelt ballads, Kaitlyn raps about touching her pussy, and she still goes on to crack the final three.

Unlike the show's usual cull of the manicured and melting-down, Kaitlyn Bristowe comes across as a grown-ass woman who knows who she is, and doesn't suffer anyone foolish enough not to get it. Faked or overstated, that stance will cut a direct path to villainy: the "I'm not here to make friends" girl. But that wasn't Bristowe's steeze. Rather, she displayed evidence of a quality that's rare in the *Bachelor* world (maybe, for that matter, the world-world): confidence that does not gorge itself on others' pain.

Another thing you need to know about Kaitlyn to understand her place in *Bachelor* franchise history: she likes sex. As in she talks about it the way you would an activity you have enjoyed in the past and would like to continue enjoying in the future:

> To me intimacy is an important part of a relationship. And I'm just not afraid to say that — I don't care what people say or think: to *me* that's important. It might not be that important to other people. But this is forever, and this is a marriage, and part of that is intimacy . . . I don't judge any person for how they go about a relationship — to each their own. If the physical part of the relationship isn't there for me, I mean, that's a deal-breaker.

In this she is not the lone representative on a *Bachelor* vanguard: others have talked, with varying degrees of explicitness, about taking sex seriously. More novel is Kaitlyn's willingness to be *un*serious about sex. This is her onscreen persona from within minutes of her arrival on set, when she exits the limo on night one and offers Farmer Chris the opportunity to "plow the fuck out of [her] field any day." When he goes speechless, she keeps up the bit, scrutinizing him cautiously: "You're not Chris? And you're not a farmer?"

Later that night, Kaitlyn does the second act of her routine for the full benefit of the group. "Why did the walrus go to the Tupperware party?" she asks the semicircle of sequins gathered to hear the Bachelor speechify about his journey. Answer: "Because he was looking for a tight seal!" Kaitlyn completes this delivery with a vaguely flipper-ish arm gesture and her go-to cackle. Every other laugh in the room has a kind of fluttering horror. Her competitors seem genuinely rattled to find such atypical *Bachelor* fare delivered in a human form as *Bachelor*-ready as Bristowe's. "Are you a tight seal?" one comedy genius asks, tentatively feeling her way into unfamiliar territory. "Duh," Kaitlyn tells her.

I'm telling you all this about Kaitlyn Bristowe because I think it's important to get a sense of the vibe she delivered to the show. Many of the hundreds of women who have appeared as contestants on *The Bachelor* have been talented, or smart, or seemed real nice, but precious few have actually just been *cool*. Kaitlyn is someone you could know in real life: she's your most irreverent yoga instructor, the girl from your middle school who was popular but not a total asshole, someone you want to have a glass of wine or four with. Her frank, jokey sex chatter brought something to *The Bachelor* that felt novel, adult, and, I have to say, really Canadian. This was a rare Bachelorette unencumbered by Puritan moral genealogy.

So, here's what happened: Kaitlyn's season, which aired in 2015, is the only one in the history of *The Bachelor* or *The Bachelorette* in which confirmed, pre–fantasy suite sex officially goes down and is folded into the season's narrative. In an act that is *Bachelor*-bold, Kaitlyn actually says the words "we had sex." The deed is done with Nick Viall, a cagey software salesman whose very presence on the show is a rule-bender: he's a past contestant[21] who turns up mid-season to make good on flirtatious social media exchanges he and Kaitlyn made pre-filming. He persuades her to let him join the pack. A couple of episodes later, they have a one-on-one date in Dublin, drink a bunch of whiskey, go back to her place, and slip into her room while their mics are still hot.

From coitus onward, the show structurally implodes. First slowly, then at an accelerated rate, like a building demolition set off by a bang sesh. Within a week, the show has added a new euphemism to its lexicon of *Bachelor*-speak: let "off-camera time" hereafter mean boning. Kaitlyn is given an injunction from Chris Harrison to cut her roster of boyfriends in half and get more of that sweet off-camera time with the remainder in order to "have an even playing field."

---

21 See his "After the Final Rose" flub with Andi, discussed earlier in this chapter.

The production schedule is rejigged: rather than proceeding to hometowns and then somewhere warm and vacation-y, the show stalls in Ireland for chilly, wind-whipped cliff dates and catch-up hookups. Kaitlyn has essentially been sentenced to remain moored on the Emerald Isle until she's fucked enough people to be allowed off it.

After having sex with Nick, Kaitlyn gets hit with what looks to me like a special hungover form of self-loathing — the kind where you wish you could reach into the recent past and vacuum up your cells. Her regrets are not, as she stresses in every sound bite "about the act," but rather because of what the deviation from the rules might mean to the other men she's dating. "I feel guilty because I do care about all of these guys," she says. "I've never done this before — I've never dated this many guys and had to feel this guilt . . . The fact that I've been intimate with Nick is not where the guilt comes from with me. The guilt comes from where my relationships are with other people." Kaitlyn feels bad because she cares about other people, not because she cares what other people think.

And for this — for feeling empathy rather than moral shame — Kaitlyn is thoroughly punished. In the "Men Tell All" suitor reunion episode, Chris Harrison pauses the usual Festivus-style airing of grievances. "This show continually pushes the boundaries," Harrison says, sans irony. "We've always had a fair amount of controversy, especially around issues of appropriate behavior, gender roles, what should and shouldn't be shown on television. These have always been issues we have embraced here on *The Bachelor*." He addresses Kaitlyn directly: "But what you're dealing with is something completely different." In front of the live studio audience, a large screen displays tweets and direct messages addressed to Kaitlyn, and Harrison reads them aloud, vocalizing the internet's worst. "Unspread your whore legs and shut your filthy, diseased mouth," he deadpans. "She should just crawl in a hole and die."

The dramatic reading has its intended effect: actually hearing these words spoken by and to a human being is shocking, and both the live audience and Kaitlyn's 20-some-odd ex-boyfriends give her a standing ovation. "I've received death threats," Kaitlyn tells Harrison. He assures her, "I would take you as a role model for my kids over anyone who would be a cyber-bully."

Ostensibly addressing real-life head-on, the show successfully transforms Kaitlyn's experience into a cyberbullying awareness campaign. But this is a slightly cynical misdirect at best, and straight-up hypocrisy at worst. Because it's not bullying that's the real problem here: it's rank, unfettered woman-hatred, and that has always formed a core part of *Bachelor* viewership.

The Bachelor's coded lexicon is a way of making exactly the "issues" Chris Harrison refers to into symbols: roses and right reasons and off-camera time become substitutes for things like appropriate behavior, gender roles, sex. *The Bachelor*'s codes further estrange signifiers from the feelings, actions, and social orders they signify. The show is at both its most fascinating and its ugliest the further it leans into that estrangement. Thing is, out there in the real(ish) world of the internet, people don't quietly admonish your off-camera time; they tell you to shut your dirty whore mouth and die.

The Bachelor and *Bachelorette*'s conservative romantic fantasy belies the fact that the show's traditions around sex are, held to a certain light, liberal ones. The regulations imposed on when and where sex happens on the show are stringent and weird, but they create a set of conditions that demand unexpectedly progressive thinking from participants. Essentially, the fantasy suite ritual asks couples to give up any possessiveness they may feel around sex and romance — to trust their partner to "explore" other relationships. It asks them to walk a path to monogamous, hyperconservative commitment that includes 11th-hour non-monogamy. If you think about it, sex on *The Bachelor* is an act of genuine pluralism. Nonetheless, as soon as someone deviates from the show's rules — no matter how arbitrary or secretly progressive those rules might be — the show's conservative base rears its ugly avatar and howls.

Chris Harrison repeatedly refers to Kaitlyn as "controversial" and her season as "polarizing." I've been thinking about those poles. *The Bachelor* has, for the last several years, wiggled around in the shady middle of a Venn diagram of conservative values and cultural relevancy. And I'm wondering whether the show still needs its truest conservative viewers to survive. I'm wondering whether in a post-Bristowe world, *The Bachelor* might just find its sweet spot and deliver an ironically sincere, spectacularly relatable spectacle for the rest of us: nasty women primed to grab ourselves by our pussies and rap.

3

Gotta Vill: Villains

Bachelor number five, NFL football player Jesse Palmer, has claim on more than one milestone of the *Bachelor* franchise. Both the show's first pro athlete and its first foreign lead (on the vanguard of a rich tradition of Canadian standouts), Palmer is probably best remembered as the only Bachelor to ever be floated a bonus rose and do-over when he flubbed his line and said the wrong woman's name in a rose ceremony. The true historical significance of Jesse's time on *The Bachelor* in 2004, however, has little to do with the man himself: the season delivered Trish Schneider, a 28-year-old model (read: unemployed person) and the earliest prototype of what would come to be, arguably, the most important role cast each season: the villain.

While the idea of being there "for the right reasons" was baked into the show's DNA from the outset[22] for six cycles over two years (four *Bachelor*, two *Bachelorette*), what the correlative "wrong reasons" might be were, in the uncharted wilderness of early gen reality TV, hazy and abstract.

Then along came Trish. She explains that she likes athletes because they're rich, promises to "capitalize" on "very pretty legs . . . that could possibly be wrapped around him," and wears a T-shirt emblazoned with the slogan "Gold Digger: Like a hooker . . . just smarter." Even after she's booted from the show, she busts up Jesse's evening with another woman and offers to pinch-hit the fantasy suite portion of the date.

And with that, *The Bachelor* discovered the power of giving living, breathing embodiment to the "bad" behavior against which the show's values had always, implicitly and imprecisely, been defined. It seemed impossible that we had ever done without this.

Because the role is not so much a character profile as it is a set of effects, there is no one way to be — or to become — a *Bachelor* or *Bachelorette* villain. Each shades the role uniquely with their particular way of being unlikeable (maybe more accurate to say "enjoyably disliked"). That said, there are recurring themes — paths that lead pretty reliably to being designated the bad guy.

---

22 I tentatively trace the iconic phrase to the inaugural season of *The Bachelorette* and to the unlikely, tangential source of Trista's stepmom.

Let's start with villainy in its bluntest form: the contestant who does not meet the show's most basic criteria of participation because they are not single. Examples include Brian on Des's season, whose girlfriend is delivered to set the third week of the show to tearfully call him out. Less dramatically, on Ben Flajnik's season of *The Bachelor*, unmemorable Casey's on-again-off-again romantic entanglement back home gets her kicked off the show, but never really earns her proper villain status, mostly due to an apparently total lack of guile: she seems to only realize she might not be in "right reasons" territory after Chris Harrison guides her there in what is supposed to read as a dramatic confrontation, but really comes across more like some low-key life coaching.

On Jake Pavelka's season of *The Bachelor*, contestant Rozlyn Papa provided a variant when, rather than keeping up a romantic attachment back in the real world, she allegedly forged one on set. She was summarily turfed three episodes into the season by Chris Harrison for the transgression of having "entered into an inappropriate relationship with one of [the show's] staffers." On "The Women Tell All," Rozlyn digs her heels in and denies the testimony of those who detail incidents of her cuddling and flirting with a producer (who was fired over the incident). One contestant goes further to say she witnessed a makeout session, and another reports that Rozlyn frequently spent the night somewhere other than her own bed. The effect of all this on Bachelor Jake and his journey is, at best, incidental. Furthermore, in a hilarious turn, somewhere along the way Rozlyn morphs from Jake's antagonist into Chris Harrison's. She fights her way off the show still throwing out personal digs at the host, accusing the then-still-married[23] Harrison of hitting on other people's wives. Harrison lets her know he wishes her well and hopes she "will become a better person."

On Jillian Harris's season of *The Bachelorette*, Wes offered another example of the villain otherwise attached. An obviously floundering country musician who spent every moment plugging his forthcoming CD,[24] Wes made it far enough to turn a hometown visit into free publicity by subjecting Jill to a concert with his band. Oh yeah, and he also had a girlfriend, I guess.

This was a weird one: about half the season was spent ineffectually addressing rumors that one of the contestants was in a relationship, a fact about which Jill seemed only nominally concerned, putting faith in her own intuition above all. There was an early *Bachelor* staginess of tone to the whole affair that makes it seem pretty clear, at least from the vantage of contemporary viewership, that the Bachelorette was in on the bit and her journey never truly threatened by Wes. The fact that she kept him on despite warnings did not dial up the drama he offered, but rather diluted the power of Wes's villainy by drawing it in cartoon form. Though Wes's motives were only ever thinly veiled at best, in his exit interview he

---

23 On the first-ever episode of the show, Harrison gestures to his ring finger to assure us that he is "a happily married man." A decade into filming, he and his wife of 18 years divorced. For more on this, I recommend Taffy Brodesser-Akner's 2015 *GQ* profile of Harrison.

24 Not album: *CD*. Just in case you were wondering whether 2009 was really such a long time ago.

comes all-the-way clean, boasting that he is "the only guy in *Bachelorette* history to make it to the top four with a girl-friend." Cue the gasps.

On Ali's season, flop Canadian wrestler Justin "Rated-R" Rego was caught leaving voicemail messages for one of his two secret girlfriends back in Ontario. Ali — who obviously had zero interest in the stunt athlete and appeared enraged purely on principle — confronted Justin, who tried to literally run away despite the hindrance of a broken leg, propelling himself away double time on a walking cast with Ali chasing him down, yelling about manhood. On its face this scene was dramatic, but on the whole Justin's storyline managed, like Wes's, to be surprisingly boring. Though he vacuumed up all his airtime selling himself as a bad boy, without even the lightest patina of nuance, Justin's attention-hungry performance was, ironically, really easy to not pay any attention to.[25]

These villains tend to be blunt, one-note, and quick to flame out. They may provide one or two confrontational set pieces to shuffle into an otherwise flatlining episode, but they rarely engender any deeply felt or long-lasting interest. Ultimately, unless they come with a little something extra (like banging a producer or needing Chris Harrison to break up with you on the Bachelor's behalf), cheater-villains are pretty forgettable figures.

There are other ways to be romantically disinterested in the show's lead that at the very least make room for novel

---

25 For what it's worth, in post-show interviews Justin claims his villain plot was constructed entirely by producers, which, if true, makes him even dumber than he seems.

content. Take Bentley Williams, who appeared on Ashley Hebert's run as Bachelorette (a season that ranks among my personal favorites). Like Wes and Justin before him, Bentley is possessed of an unmistakable, ham-fisted, in-your-face duplicity. In interviews with producers, he is openly hostile to the idea of dating Ashley (she is "just not [his] type") but he nonetheless makes a sport of trying to capture her attention. By just a couple of episodes into the season, he already has (poor, sweet, gullible) Ashley falling hard while, behind her back, he delivers such gems as "I would literally rather be swimming in pee than trying to plan a wedding with her." At the very least, Bentley's cruelty came with some creativity of expression. That said, his mumbly, adolescent affect had about all the charm of a sk8r boi's sweat sock, making Ashley's infatuation with him sort of hard to sign off on.

Like Jillian Harris, Ashley had to "la-la-la I can't hear you" through a lot of warnings on her villain's behalf. She was contacted pre-filming by a mutual acquaintance[26] warning that Bentley's intentions were nefarious, his presence on the show merely some vague promotion of his "business." Like Jill before her, Ashley opted to trust her own judgment instead of heeding these cautions. Unlike Jill, she appeared genuinely emotionally harrowed by her villain's seduction and exit, making the odds that she was involved in the ploy seem unlikely.

It's worth noting that the Bachelorette trope of the villain-as-Machiavellian-businessman does not exist on The Bachelor,

---

26 Michelle Money: former Bachelor contestant with a future both on the Pad and as a rare bird of Paradise.

where women are never credited with professional motivations. Rather than being shown to exploit the show for specific, practical reasons, they are ascribed vague goals like seeking "attention." The show endorses a cliché that men want money and women want fame — a truism that, of course, ignores the complex ways the two are bound on unscripted television.

Regardless, there are a couple of things to learn from the franchise's middle-era male villains (Jillian, Ali, and Ashley were Bachelorettes five through seven). This was an unsubtle villainy — contestants who cast themselves as baddy-bads in private interviews, planting revelations set to go off only upon broadcast. The ultimate goal appears not so much to come off well, but to pull something off. (Remember, this was a less social-media-evolved era, in which the idea that any publicity was "good" had not yet fallen into categorical obsolescence.) Like Wes congratulating himself on being the first non-single Bachelor to make top four, when Bentley opts to send himself home, he crows (well, it would be crowing if Bentley's voice didn't sound the way bad posture looks) over having fooled "these freaking idiots" with his shenanigans. He goes on: "She's more into me than anyone else, but none of them have any idea that I don't care about Ashley. I had the opportunity, and I played everyone. That's something that's never been done before."

So, one way to be a villain is to signal a lack of authentic romantic interest: to be "not there for [the lead]." But the opposite is equally a path to villainy: being *only* there for the lead. This premise forms the logical core of a true reality TV classic, a motto I would submit with "they misunderestimated me" as among the defining phrases of the aughts: *I'm not here to make friends.*

In this model, we have a parade of villains who have made for some of the franchise's most enduring figures: Courtney on Ben Flajnik's season, Michelle Money[27] on Brad's (his second go-around), Ben on Desiree's, Tierra on Sean's, Vienna on Jake's, Nick on Andi's, Olivia on Ben Higgins's. It would be impossible to detail all the many glorious moments these characters delivered — each one truly, specially love-hateable in his or her own way.

Those in this long and memorable line are more likely than their earlier counterparts to be massaged into villainy by production rather than delivering it themselves with a bow, à la Bentley, Wes, and the like. Their apparent degree of participation in their own typecasting varies. Some, like Tierra for example, seem to cast a wide and deliberate net of manipulation, putting on a show for the audience as much as for the Bachelor. I shit you not, in her seven-episode run, Tierra pulled off staging a fake medical emergency *more than one time* (say what you will about T., that's some chutzpah). Her signature look — a variant on the resting bitch face featuring a rogue, arch-prone eyebrow — may have been beyond her control, but her signature promise to never lose "her sparkle" was a calculated, hashtag-baiting performance.

Other villains seem more victims of their personality and

---

27 An icon of the type where it's impossible to use only her first name. She is always Michelle Money.

its chemical interaction with the unholy *Bachelor* cocktail of competition and communal living. Those like, say, Olivia Caridi, Nick Viall, and Courtney Robertson get their villainy on with a combo of competitive intensity and lack of fraternal social grace. These characters are often early front-runners who don't play nice with others, tending to mistake oxygen-vacuuming ambition for keeping an eye on the prize.

Officially, of course, it's not against the rules to "focus on your relationship" with the lead at the expense of others. Unofficially, it's a great way to guarantee negative attention, which is a great way to threaten your odds of success. Though, it must be said, sometimes these overly competitive tactics do in the strictest sense work: there have been seasons when the villain proves the victor. But when this happens, it's a sign that somewhere along the way the balance of the season has skewed away from romance and into game show. In these cases, the resulting relationships have not just failed, they've been full-scale, public dumpster fires (see: Jake and Vienna, Courtney and Ben). Villains can be winners, but they're never true-lovers.

Here's another irony of villainy: though it can be accompanied by an irreverent lack of regard for the show's official and unofficial rules, it can also come by way of failing to plausibly deny knowledge of how the show works. Namely, you're going to get hit with a hardcore case of the villains in your edit if you show any glimmer of thought to the show's cyclical nature and the fact that the next Bachelor or Bachelorette is usually cast from among late-stage rejects. So you're damned if you don't attend to the short game and make friends, but you're also damned if you attend to the long game and think in any practical terms about what — other than an engagement — making it far on the show might offer.

On Des's season, James learned this the hard way and was saddled with a brief, two-episode stint as villain after he was overheard making an off-the-cuff comment about his Bachelor casting odds while shooting the shit with another contestant about trawling for women back home (the latter strikes me as more of a problem than the former, but on the show, these were treated as equally damning). Similarly, Kaitlyn's suitor Ian, if not exactly narratively enticing enough to be a full-on villain, secured himself as persona non grata in Bachelor Nation by making an explicit play for lead in his exit interview: "If I was made Bachelor, I think they would come out of the woodwork, man. I think they'd be like, 'Oh shit, I wanna go out with that guy. He's so deep.'"[28]

I can't help coming back to the fact that being a contestant on *The Bachelor* asks much more of a person — intellectually, emotionally, and, dare I say, spiritually — than we might commonly allow. Contestants must submit fully to the logic of the show's machinations, internalizing its contradictions so completely that the patent absurdities become something they can rise above, train themselves to ignore. It's an act of immersion, of surrender. It's faith: to leap over a chasm of reason and

---

28 On "The Men Tell All," though, Ian quite literally threw himself to the ground in apologetic surrender, lowering himself to become fruit hung too low to hate. It was pathetic and highly effective.

deliver oneself to some peace, denying the apparent truth of one's reality.[29] All this to say, to win the show you must always remember your place; and yet to truly fall in love, you must grant yourself the respite to forget where you are. Sometimes villains are simply those would-be front-runners who fail at this magical thinking.

One thing all varietals of villain share is that while they occasionally (although rarely) score an ally or two, they are by and large disliked by the other contestants. In fact, someone getting on other peoples' nerves often represents the first germinal winks of a villain being born. The villain's storyline is as much about intrahouse dynamics as it is about their relationship to the lead.

Then again, sometimes a contestant is unpopular, but no amount of cajoling from editing and production will a villain make. On Ashley Hebert's season, for example, there was Ryan, a sustainable-something-or-other entrepreneur whose "positive energy" earned him the first impression rose. Ryan was, indeed, pretty goddamn positive. He seemed like he was living in a TED Talk.[30] His joyful enthusiasm was apparently genuine — or at least it was impossible to chip into even under the duress of *Bachelor*-produced conditions, which more or less amounts to the same thing. Ryan bounded around the

29 In this case "reality" being the reality that you are making reality TV.

30 I'd bet money he keeps a "Be the Change" poster hanging over his desk.

71

Bachelor set like a golden retriever, not noticing what he was bashing into and whose feet he was getting under. The guys hated him because he was such a try-hard. Ashley liked him because he was so nice.

It's hard to oversell just how thoroughly Ryan was disliked for someone no one could really justify a bad word about. A few episodes in, just considering the prospect of Ryan getting a group date rose, one contestant promises to throw himself off their sky-scraping Hong Kong hotel. Through teeth-gritted diplomacy, Blake describes Ryan as "easy to get along with . . . in small doses" before going on to admit that the exuberance is intolerable.

As other *Bachelor* contestants tend to do with villains, Blake frames the Ryan problem through a series of logical premises aimed to locate Ashley's romantic taste and clarify his own self-image: "If we're there, and Ryan's there, how can she see anything with us . . . because he's completely different . . . We just have fundamental differences. If Ryan gets the rose tonight I would be livid. I would probably just pack up and go home." Self-talk exactly like this comes up pretty much every season — "if she likes him, she cannot also like me, because I am not like him" — it's just that usually it's about villains, not nice-guy keeners.

Similarly, future Bachelor Ben Flajnik feels that "everybody wants Ashley to see Ryan for who he really is." Here we have another *Bachelor* trope typically used to accuse contestants of villainy: projecting a false persona to mask wrong reasons behind the façade of right ones. But the problem with

Ryan is not that he is disingenuous; it's that he's cloyingly earnest. He's practically the official Right Reasons poster boy. Ben is equating the "real Ryan" with his social standing. He's not talking about being honest — he's talking about being cool.

Ryan offers a case study of a villain workaround. Ashley's original villain, Bentley, wrote himself off the show too quickly.[31] With no understudy left in his stead, and the house's least-popular dude seemingly made of negativity Teflon, rather than push a storyline unlikely to graft, the show generates an *effect* of villainy rather than forcing the appearance of the usual cause. The right narrative is still in reach, with suspense generated as the house waits for the lead to catch up to a truth they — and we — are privy to. And as it turns out, Ryan didn't need to be a bad guy to get some mileage out of him. Functionally speaking, being a faker and being a loser amount to the same thing.

As I alluded to in Chapter 1, the exploitation of one's "story" is a consummate *Bachelor* sin. Of all villain-makers — even more than outright rule-breaking disqualifiers like pre-existing romantic attachments — overselling a sad tale is the single behavior contestants and viewers most violently despise and readily punish.

On Des's season of *The Bachelorette*, for example, there's

---

31 Though his specter haunted her journey for several more weeks, Bentley's in-the-flesh villainy had a mere three-episode run. He was also allotted a brief cameo return that involved schlepping him all the way to Hong Kong to give the pining Bachelorette some closure, whereupon Ashley tweaked immediately to his thorough douchery, and her journey to find love elsewhere was successfully salvaged.

Ben: a bar owner and divorced dad from Texas who front-loads his "story" by sending his pint-sized offspring out of the limo in his stead. Her ovaries surely aflame, Des rewards this parenthood pageantry with the first impression rose.

But Ben's drawling southern sweetness wears out its welcome in the house real quick. Within an episode or two, the other men call out his pining dad schtick as a sham. They take particular note of the fact that while Ben never mentions his actual progeny, he does talk of plans for his business to go forth and multiply, citing past Bachelors who have used the show's publicity to expand ownership of one bar into five.[32] The men speculate that Ben's fatherhood is largely of the absentee variety,[33] and the idea that he is using his sad-dad story to gain traction with Des enrages them.

A classic *Bachelor* move: send the lead on a two-on-one date with the villain and the housemate most righteously turnt up about said villain's existence. (Even if the latter wins the battle, the fact of being so fixated on righting injustices in the behavior of others is a guarantee they will never conquer the war. As far back as I can get data, no two-on-one date victor has ever come off the show engaged.)

---

32 Ben is thinking here of Brad Womack, who famously picked no one on his first kick at the can and scored a do-over season.

33 The house compares Ben's behavior to fellow dad contestant Juan Pablo, who, apparently, will not shut up about his daughter. Originally from Venezuela, former pro-soccer player Juan Pablo would wind up the dark horse next Bachelor, but at this point in Des's season, the fact that he talks at length about *anything* is a surprise to viewers, who have heard his voice so rarely that the question of whether or not he speaks English at all remains on the table. Ultimately, the fact that no one knew anything about Juan Pablo except that his accent was sexy resulted in him becoming the most universally reviled Bachelor of all time. I'm probably in a minority of one for kinda-sorta not entirely hating Juan Pablo's season. Go figure.

In this case, the self-styled champion of honor (Des's, the show's, the world's) is Michael, a Chicago attorney who promises to go pro on Ben's false storytelling: "I do have certain trial tactics when it comes to cross-examining and impeaching someone who is not telling the truth. So today Ben will be found guilty of fraud and impersonation of a southern gentleman. I'm ready to send this fucker home." In addition to just being a generally too keyed up kind of guy, Michael's personal history with an absentee dad has him particularly riled. He winds up taking his evisceration too far, and though Des heeds the warning and sends Ben home, Michael is booted the following week. (You'll remember from Chapter 1: Des likes to keep things positive.)

Though Ben was universally disliked for his telling of tales, he would prove to be but a shadow of the villain born of too much story. The ultimate, all-time, never-to-be-topped paragon of this character arrived two years later, on Chris Soules's season, in the form of contestant Kelsey Poe.

We were cued early on to watch Kelsey closely: in episode one, the montage previewing Chris's harem-to-be lingered long on the 27-year-old high school guidance counsellor. On a season that was all beachy waves and Kardashian-era contours and highlights, Kelsey stood out with her chin-length bob, tank-top-cardigan sets, and *Bachelor*-relative lack of makeup. She had the old-fashioned, near-missable prettiness of a girl who might morph from next-door normal to timeless beauty somewhere between blinks. With perfectly pitched, emotional-but-controlled narration, Kelsey tells us she was widowed less than a year and a half prior when her husband unexpectedly dropped dead of a heart attack. From the vantage of hindsight it seems hard to imagine, but in these first glimpses of footage — being all profesh at her job, meditating on love and loss, going for a sweat-free jog — Kelsey came off as grounded, mature, and a romantic kind of sad. She looked like a real contender.

Where were the first hints that something was off? On a lakeside camping date a few episodes in, while the rest of the group frolicks happily, Kelsey gripes to producers about being stuck at a "dingy pond" on a "date made for bimbos." When fun-loving Kaitlyn Bristowe moons everyone as she leaps into the water ("He saw my tush!" she boasts later), Kelsey declares it "not appropriate . . . I think if you have dignity and you're self-respecting this is the moment when you just want to call it quits." And thus Kelsey's old-timey reserve is revealed to be not so much in the style of 19th-century heroine-in-mourning as 21st-century humorless prude.

The other women remark that Kelsey is "out of her element" and "pouting like I've never seen someone pout before." They observe how in Chris's presence "all of a sudden happy Kelsey is out." To her credit, Kelsey would not disagree: "My face is getting skinnier because I spend too much time fake-smiling trying to pretend to enjoy this hellhole. There are moments where I feel like taking a fork and stabbing it in my eye," she says. She declares the whole experience "questionable," and is promptly stung in the crotch by a wasp.

It's tough to cover for pissiness on *The Bachelor*. The show has an extremely low threshold for anything like negativity or ingratitude. When you whinge and sulk in private and then turn on your sunbeams for the benefit of the lead, you aren't a good sport tamping down a touch of grouchiness — you're a two-faced viper conspiring to defraud the hero and his pure-hearted entourage out of true love. Kelsey's inability to join in is no exception: "I think that Kelsey is phoney-baloney," Ashley Iaconetti says. "I just catch the extreme fake vibe. Fake smile, fake laugh." (She then throws her head back and does a not-off-base imitation of Kelsey's diaphragmatic ha's.)

It's one of those things where, when you've stepped to the side and taken in a new angle on something, it's hard to roll back and see things in fewer dimensions. Once you notice how painfully mannered Kelsey is, it suffuses her every second onscreen. How was it possible to ever *not* hear that Kelsey speaks with the overenunciated locution of a drama major telegraphing the influence of a continental semester abroad? Or the strained way she plucks words from the furthest ken of her vocabulary like a freshman composition paper brought to life? (Some choice bits: "It was an emotionally tumultuous day . . . flooded, like when there are too many emotions amassing"; "I had no control over my motor movements"; "A flippant comment was misconstrued as condescending, but if someone had expressed to me something that I said, I would have ameliorated it.")

But the only person who calls out Kelsey's "big words" is Kelsey. The other women aren't bothered by how she speaks, but by what she says. They note that she is "not very nice" and "makes these snide comments" that hurt other people's feelings. When confronted, Kelsey feigns shame and apology, but in private she appraises the situation thusly: "I get it. I'm blessed with eloquence, and I'm articulate, and I use a lot of big words. Because I'm smart. I didn't go through all this shit — death of a spouse, loss in numerous, numerous ways — to get ganged up on by girls in the house."[34]

By episode five, Kelsey is elevated from pretentious annoyance to housewide archfiend. Sensing that she is at risk of not continuing on, she steals away to Chris's room before a rose ceremony to parlay her widowhood into romantic connection, maneuvering his sympathetic bear hug into an uncomfortable makeout. She declares the "rose ceremony canceled — he's made up his mind" while Chris laughs awkwardly and attempts to disentangle.

It's not uncommon for someone who is disliked by the group to slip in off-schedule time with the lead (their ability to locate his or her whereabouts surely a boost from producers, who know a good line on drama when they see one). So though Kelsey is, as she says "stealing this time," until this point, nothing about her behavior has strayed beyond the pale of *Bachelor* villain fare. But here she zags into uncharted territory. In the post-game following her confession, she brings her hands to her chest with a satisfied sigh and gushes: "Isn't my story amazing? It's *tragic* — but it's amazing. I *love* my

---

34 Hey, listen, as a person who's been on the receiving end of more than one "big words" shaming from packs of girls in my day (shout out to the soccer teams of early pubescence!), I might have sympathized on this one. In my experience, though, what's humiliating about being mocked for it is that if you come to your rangy vocab by honest, inalienable nerdiness, you probably aren't trying to sound smart — you're trying to sound just like everyone else. And when attention is called to the fact that you don't, you feel unfit to exist in public.

story." And she goes on, bringing this thought to a *Bachelor*-unbelievable (or just, like, normal-life unbelievable) conclusion: "I know this is a show about Chris, but this is my love story too. This is the unfolding of somebody who's been through something *so* tragic, and you get to watch her pick up the pieces and grow into another person and into another relationship. And I'm so glad that the first kiss is something that can be written in the storybooks. And hell yes I'm getting a rose tonight! Stay tuned. Monday nights at eight. The love story unveiled."

As I said in Chapter 1, there comes a point in the season's arc when each contestant must imagine that their story and the lead's have merged and are heading for the same, fated end. What I did not say — because it goes without saying — is that it is not within the realm of *Bachelor* logic that any contestant should recast themselves as the show's protagonist. When she ends her monologue with a little flourish of her hand on "unveiled," it's as though Kelsey is quite literally parting the fourth wall like a curtain, crossing over to a remote, quasi-meta reality TV plane. Here she transforms into something new: a monstrous hybrid of self-consciousness and a total inability to conceive of how she is perceived by others.

Though the other women in the house will not hear this particular sound bite until the show airs, they chafe plenty at Kelsey's public behavior. In the hours following her stolen storytime, Kelsey loses her grip on all decorum, boasting a confidence that seems, from the perspective of the other women (who do not know she's seen Chris alone) unearned. She goes so far as to suggest that she will be sad to bid adieu to one of them by evening's end.

When Chris cancels the cocktail party, citing the emotional taxation of Kelsey's sad story (outing her for sneaking in the alone time), she faints and has a panic attack, earning her time with both the on-set medic and, at her request, Chris. Even the gentlest among the women are skeptical, believing this to be "a tactical move" to earn even more ill-begotten minutes in the Bachelor's presence. "The past has shown us that Kelsey has a tragic story and uses it at the right times," one says. "I think we're all trying to figure out what part of her is real and what part of this is manipulative," says another. Another is more bold: "She's completely full of shit."

If Kelsey's behavior is indeed strategic, it works. She gets a rose, and two other women are booted. As one contestant summarizes: "Kelsey was probably going home tonight, and she went to Chris's room and she told this story, and now somebody else is going home. And she did that. She did that on purpose." Final four and future *Paradise* staple Jade Roper[35] points to what she perceives as a specific one-to-one injustice regarding the fate of a contestant eliminated in Kelsey's stead: "Sam, she's had terrible things happen to her too that's shaped the person who she is. But she didn't use it as, like, a level-up." Kaitlyn Bristowe adds: "I wanted to punch her in the teeth-holder. It's not about your sad story anymore — it's about you being a shitty human being."

35 Now Jade Tolbert, having since met and married her husband, Tanner, under the watch of *Bachelor in Paradise*.

Notice that all Kelsey-related complaints relate in some way to her use of story. Some contestants go so far as to doubt its veracity entirely: "What if she's lying about the husband thing?" Ashley I. laughs, seemingly in jkjk mode until she sees the producer's reaction offscreen. "You think that may be a possibility, don't you?" she asks, turning theatrically serious. "Do you have actual paperwork?"

The next episode, Ashley and Kelsey are sent on a two-on-one date to the Badlands of South Dakota (Kelsey boasts about her superior knowledge of geography for being able to distinguish between the Badlands and the Black Hills, and as they fly over Mount Rushmore, she chirpily IDs the presidents like a Reach for the Top contestant). Ashley spills the beans about Kelsey's unanimously despised status in the house to Chris, who pulls the little-used but baller move of dispensing with both women by the end of the date. Even in her exit interview, Kelsey continues to blow the *Bachelor* storytelling game apart: "My story is amazing: it's tragic, and it's inspiring, and it's beautiful. I am immeasurably blessed."

This last sound bite is apparently a Kelsey catchphrase: back at the hotel, when the other women see her suitcase dragged off, they scream, jump on the furniture, and douse a row of glasses with something piss-colored and sparkling to raise to being "*all* immeasurably blessed." On past seasons, contestants may have gloated over a villain's departure, but a full-service, unanimous victory dance of this kind is unprecedented.

Kelsey was a model of the inadvertent villain — her anti-social behavior a reflection, I believe, of an authentic lack of self-awareness, not one adopted to exploit the show's attention.[36] In order to accommodate the overflow of interest generated by Kelsey's uniquely revealing villainy, the show goes on to add a mid-season, behind-the-scenes bonus episode that includes a one-on-one chat with Kelsey and host Chris Harrison. "You became one of the most controversial women in the house," he tells her.

"Am I really that controversial?" she asks, pronouncing it *contra-ver-see-al*.

Harrison, who has witnessed the ritualistic fêting of her departure, deadpans, "I think so."

The Bachelor demands that all contestants employ some degree of strategy, but it abhors anyone who reveals themselves to *be* a strategist. This is not a casual hypocrisy, but an integral element of the show's structure. As I've written elsewhere in this book, the whole idea that there are right reasons for arriving on the set of *The Bachelor* amounts to a category error. And yet it is crucially important that the show cultivates the notion that some of the behavior it captures is, in fact, "right." The villain is an emissary sent to chart the outer limits of the

---

36 The most damning evidence that Kelsey's was not a made-for-TV pathology comes off-camera and pre-*Bachelor*: in a truly bizarre obituary she appears to have penned for her deceased husband, she pivots his eulogy into an unalloyed celebration of her own accomplishments that reads like a darkly comic curriculum vitae. And hey, people do weird things when grieving that they should be forgiven for, but this little factoid certainly does seem to be in step with her self-aggrandizing story chatter on the show.

show's comfort with performance by transgressing its final boundary, showing us precisely what too much looks like. He or she offers a coordinate by which we may triangulate authenticity in a landscape that is, unavoidably, inauthentic. The villain's demonstration of "bad" allows the other characters' "good" to be made visible. The villain is a reference — a relief.

Rather than remain the flat surface of foil, however, the *Bachelor* and *Bachelorette* villain is multidimensional, can be folded like an origami basket: a place for viewers to comfortably store our biggest, most unwieldy emotional reactions. *The Bachelor* is designed to generate higher-order feelings (true love, pure hate) through lower-order means (the surveillance and spectacle of human beings). In this process, the villain is the ultimate scapegoat, less than subtly bearing the brunt of the show's subtleties, contradictions, and complications. He or she takes the fall for the entirety of the show's artifice. In short: we hate the villain for being fake so we can love *The Bachelor* for making love real.

But here's the sly truth the show keeps us from looking at directly (are you ready for it?): the real villain of *The Bachelor* or *Bachelorette* is, and as always been, the hero, the man or woman of the hour, the lead.

Think about it. As we know, *The Bachelor* is a show built on contradictions. Its two forms — love story and game show — give rise to conflicting-yet-entwined goals: for the hero to find true love, and to lead on as many people as possible for as long as possible. And while the former may demand emotional honesty and vulnerability from the show's central figure, the latter is less flattering. Spins on truth, lies of omission, thinking one thing but behaving so as to suggest the opposite: this is the bare minimum of duplicity the show will require of its love object. And the bar may be pushed much higher to include moves from every hue on the asshole-to-sociopath spectrum: emotionally involving someone's family, accepting professions of love under false pretenses, delivering lines that front-load rejection with false encouragement, sitting through full-length marriage proposals intending to turn them down. This is what it takes to be the Bachelor or Bachelorette. To dodge these parts of the role would be to break the rules, ruin the fun for the rest of us.

There's a moment nearly every season when the lead breaks down (there are often tears involved), suffering a realization usually articulated as something like: "this is harder than I thought it would be." In their former lives as viewers and participants, they likely labored under the illusion that Bachelors and Bachelorettes are rewarded for good intentions and good behavior — that the journey to true love is an honest one. In fact, the lead's job is to *never* be entirely honest. Embarking on a "journey to find love" means getting to be less the hero and more a villain hidden in plain sight. Playing Bachelor is so hard because it is so cruel.

The designated villain distracts from all this by delivering the show's highest moments of tension, drama, and — Chris Harrison's favorite word — controversy. By appearing to antagonize the hero's journey to true love, they reinforce the notion that this journey is a noble one, redirecting any latent aggression the show may provoke in viewers or contestants away from the producers, the cameras, the setup, and, of course, the hero.

There's a reason villains so often carry stories just a frame off from the one that might elect another season's Bachelor or Bachelorette, why they are often thirsty to play lead, why they may go down still insisting their story could be a great one if they were only graced with a little good light. There is something elemental, almost mythic at work here: the hero is the villain — the villain the fall-man parody. The two roles are locked into a kind of spiritually twinned antagonism: a before-and-after portrait of the fallen angel, a dot of yin buried, deep and codependent, in the yang.

I see distinct strata running through an archaeology of *Bachelor* villainy. Early villains tended to be crudely cut parodies who signalled their intentions to the camera, styling themselves as masterminds of their own antagonism. Watching back from a perspective attuned to more nuanced forms of gamesmanship, these villains tend to look pretty ridiculous. But they provided a sketch to fill in with finer details, a foundation for the role's evolution.

The timeline is not a straight shot, but in fits and starts the show went on to accumulate a lineage of characters who seemed as though they might represent the *Bachelor* villain settling into its final state: ambiguous, by turns attractive and repulsive, forged with varying degrees of intentionality. More likely than their predecessors to have their roles made or tweaked in the editing room, this breed is also more apt to show subtle knowledge of how the series works and what they stand to gain from its attentions.

While this type — what I think of as the *Bachelor* villain in its classical form — has not yet gone extinct, I submit that we are now witnessing a new movement, the nascent lapping of a third wave of villainy that promises to blend the caricature of the first cohort of villains with the media-comfy *Bachelor*-literacy of the second. More and more, we are seeing *Bachelor* and *Bachelorette* villains who are dumb but savvy, self-referential but post-ironic, who instinctively aim their antagonism not at the hero's journey, but at the show's formal structures. This villain is less Doctor Evil and more 4chan. The villain as troll.

Though she does not embody the type herself, Kelsey Poe's love affair with her own story was an earth-scorching that exposed the fertile ground in which the New Villain has germinated. Kelsey ran down a well-trod *Bachelor* path not only to its logical end, but well past it. By calling attention to the function of sob stories on the show, she cleared way for something novel: villainy that does not suicide like a stray balloon gone too far aloft when it approaches meta territory.

Enter JJ and Clint, two of Kaitlyn's suitors on the subsequent season of *The Bachelorette*. Both start out as standard bearers of mid-level contender doofus-legitimacy,[37] but by only a few episodes in, their paths change course as it becomes clear they are more invested in becoming frosh-week-style besties with one another than finding love. Clint declares their fratty bond "a success story," admitting that his homosocial affection for JJ runs deeper than any romantic attachment to Kaitlyn.[38]

Having secured their douche simpatico, Clint and JJ conspire to do whatever it takes — even behave villainously — in order to remain together as the last two standing. Though it was not aired in an episode proper, in B-roll footage that appears among the teasers and bonuses offered online by ABC, we see Clint and JJ scheme to separate themselves from contestants who are, as JJ puts it, "the background noise — the extras to our love story." As they analyze the show's moving parts, they arrive at a conclusion I may have earnestly spun a couple hundred words on myself.

CLINT: It's funny how similar the hero and the villain are.

JJ: It's scary. Sometimes you wonder if they're the *same*.

Leaning into "same" with a blend of sincerity and piss-takery, JJ is delivering the germ of a new kind of villainy — one that,

37 If you haven't already seen it, please, please do yourself a favor immediately and go watch the group date in episode 3 where the men get stand-up comedy advice from Amy Schumer. Her interaction with JJ is amazing.

38 The show did a whole "Brokeback Bachelor" marketing thing around this storyline that was really obnoxious.

rather than merely threatening the lead, hectors the roles and structures of the show itself.

Knowing he is at risk of going home, Clint sets out to seduce Kaitlyn in hopes of staying on to pal around the pool and open bar. His take on the kiss they share is delivered to producers in troll-speak: "I was wearing my power socks, so I felt like I had the power, and I had to just abuse it." Clint reports back to JJ, who surmises, "If the eyepatch fits, you gotta wear it." Clint responds by raising his drink in toast, "Villains gotta vill." Their whiskey tumblers meet to chime in a new age of *Bachelor* villain.

The call was heard, and the villains answered. On Nick Viall's season in 2017, for example, Corinne Olympios flounces into the mansion like she's doing a highlight reel of *Bachelor* villains past in the form of a one-woman show. Corinne is baiting, and indiscriminate about it: she's a 24-year-old who runs a "multi-million-dollar company," and she still has a nanny, and she's ready for marriage, and her "vagine is platinum," and she wants you to know all of it. And she'll interrupt and break rules and strip down and if you don't like it, maybe she'll own you in a fight, or maybe she'll just take a nap.

Channeling a common quality of *Bachelor* villains, Corinne is (at least ostensibly) very sexually frank. But the sexuality she reveals is studied and strange. It's either more *Bachelor* parody, or just flat-out childish: whipped cream and bouncy castles and surprise nudity. It's Veruca Salt after reading back issues of *Maxim*.

Like more and more contestants these days, Corinne has come of age in a world in which *The Bachelor* has always existed, and the villainy she achieves has an unstudied, born-with-it-ness. It's a villainy that cannot help but reference itself, a villainy fated to postmodern pastiche. Corinne calls our attention to the ways the role is structural. Though she reveals herself to be increasingly (and surprisingly charmingly) idiosyncratic, on the whole, her performance is less a character and more a fact — a part of the machinery.

The best example of the new villain, though, is Chad on JoJo's season of *The Bachelorette*, who embodies the part with what I can only describe as a kind of Nietzschean übermenschiness. Freed from the constraints of *Bachelor* morality, Chad nagged JoJo's suitors for submitting to the show's illogic like a gadfly on steroids.[39] When the first date cards come in and contestants express requisite disappointment at not being named, Chad points out, "You've gone a full life of not seeing JoJo. You can't wait, like, a day? You can chill — she'll be here. She's not going to disappear next week. She's not going to get on a jet and fly away to Malaysia."

His critique aggressively inserts an artifact of real-world logic. To go far on the show, you must play the game only well enough to permit yourself to forget that you are playing. Chad is an aggro, nagging reminder — both to the other men and to

---

39 Quite literally: a major part of Chad's storyline is the not-at-all-unlikely accusation that his emotional instability is a result of 'roid rage. This comes from nebbish Evan Bass, an owner of male impotence clinics, whose diagnosis is not an uneducated one. At the suggestion, Chad grabs Evan by the shirt hard enough to rip it and then later punches a door. Or, in his words, "The door walked into the way of my hand."

the viewers — of the surrender to something contrived. When he looks around the first morning in the house and points out the fact that "every guy here seems to be obsessed with JoJo already," he is holding himself apart from *Bachelor* standard operating procedure. We know he can never go far because he's failing to even arrive on the playing field; he may, however, throw some jams in the smooth-running cogs of a journey or two before he leaves. Or he may just punch someone out.

Chad participates in a group date in which the hosts of ESPN's *SportsNation* (recast as *BachelorNation*) power-rank the contestants based on the results of a series of challenges (get puke-risk dizzy and propose to JoJo, do an end zone dance, etc.). Goofy, embarrassing, a little stupid: this is typical early-in-the-season stuff in which, the competition for one-on-one time notwithstanding, the only way to really lose is to be a bad sport.

Chad can't deal. And he can't resist calling out those who can. He has words for everyone involved. To JoJo: "If you're going to ask me all the things I love about you, I don't know yet. I mean these guys can all tell you all the different things that they love about you and they've studied about you on TV or whatever, but I don't know." To the group: "You all can't be in love with her. If you are, that's weird. And what's to stop you from falling in love with the next girl who walks up? This is the first beautiful girl you've ever seen?" To Jordan Rodgers, eventual season winner:[40] "Forgive me if I'm not going to be

---

40 As of writing, he and JoJo are still engaged.

fake. I'm not an actor. You look like you are right now.[41] That's cool, do your thing."

In each of these examples, Chad is saying something that is completely true, but also, in a universe governed by *Bachelor*-think, completely beside the point. By taking the premise of each challenge literally, he draws attention to the fact that it is, in fact, a challenge — a game. One that does not measure, by any real-world metric, romantic suitability. And thus he reframes the other contestants' playing by the rules as being untruthful.

The group date competition is a microcosm of the show. And now, rather than being the villain whose existence plots a point on the outer reaches of contrivance by which we might recognize and admire the authenticity of other characters, Chad stubbornly positions himself as a coordinate of authenticity that threatens to expose the contrivance of the universe in which he turns. He jump-starts stakes by threatening not just JoJo's journey, or Jordan's, but the viewer's. His villainy tests the mettle of our ability to believe that a game show can produce love.

As much as Chad used seriousness as a kind of reality-bomb threat to the show's logic, he was also, with the anarchic spirit

---

41 Jordan, with his celebrity-ready hair, is an interesting example of how star-makery has made "right reasons" obsolete. Himself a not-so-successful but working pro football player (NFL downgraded to CFL), Jordan also happens to be the younger brother of the world's most successful living athlete, Green Bay Packers quarterback Aaron Rodgers. With Jordan's practice-squad career ended by injury, he came to *The Bachelorette* an out-of-work late-20-something with celebrity experience and telegenic good looks. He was clearly the contestant best prepared for life after the show — the best candidate for the job of winning. That may sound like a mercenary assessment, but isn't marriage fundamentally mercantile? Isn't it also a way of saying that it's a good match?

of a troll, definitely fucking around. Whenever he was not violently angry,[42] he kept up a waggish smirk, and in both speech and action revealed a loose, halfway accidental genius for the absurd. He plows through cocktail parties stuffing his face with cold cuts ("He would take an IV of meat if he could get one," another contestant notes). During a conversation with his sometimes-ally Canadian fitness model Daniel,[43] Chad chows down a sweet potato whole, biting it like an apple. He delivers such aphorisms as "Like I've said all along: I'm going to say what I want to say and when I want to say it" and "Life ain't all blueberries and paper airplanes, you know what I mean?"

Chad's flair for creative expression cranks into particularly high gear when he is moved to insult. In appraising his competition, he shows a predilection for simile ("These guys are acting like wrinkly, worn-out-looking high school kids"), allusion ("It was like if the Care Bears surrounded you and told you they were going to kick your ass," and "It was like watching *West Side Story* — a bunch of dudes [*demonstrates snapping*] around me"), and compellingly mixed metaphor ("If you're making a protein shake made of the group of dudes here, and, you know, blended it up . . . half that dude-protein-shake would have zero chance with JoJo").

---

42 And though I'm reading a lot of Chad's behavior as expressions of the absurd, I don't mean to overlook that violence. Later, in Chad's very brief appearance on *Bachelor in Paradise*, some of the qualities that made him, at least for a little while, a good-time villain veer into abuse and misogyny.

43 Who will turn up on *Paradise* to prove himself a quasi-genius of figurative expression in his own right.

Before I leave Chad for good,[44] a final note regarding his human form. Chad is possessed of the kind of overstimulated bulk that requires a huge amount of time, energy, and planning to maintain. It's the difference between being a person who gets exercise and eats food, and being a body that takes work and needs fuel. Chad's physical body and its appetites are the common denominator across both halves of his villain's countenance: the rageaholic jonesing to beat his way into domination, and the shit-eating joker with an on-point but unrefined instinct for satire. *The Bachelorette* is hardly a stranger to musclebound workout fiends,[45] but Chad is truly something else. Not because he is biggest or strongest or most gym-ratty, but because he makes himself most undeniable. After Chad is sent home,[46] the house performs last rites[47] with a leftover jug of one of his many protein powders, casting handfuls of Chad's very lifeblood to the wind like so many ashes to ashes, dust to dust.

44 That's a lie: we'll return to Chad in Chapter 6 when we go to *Paradise*.

45 I'd take the high side of an over-under bet on the number of dudes on Des's season who were in some phase of cycling on or off performance enhancers at, like, ten.

46 Speaking of bodies, the self-appointed, fired-up nemesis who bumps Chad off by winning their two-on-one date is Alex, a no-neck marine who can't be more than five-foot-five and has one of the most transparent Napoleon complexes I've ever seen.

47 This ritualization licensed, no doubt, by the Kelsey Poe departure.

4

It's Like a Real-Life Thing: Production

A disclaimer: this chapter has no inside sources. I did not interview, interrogate, chat with, or in any other manner engage anyone who produces *The Bachelor* about what they do or how they do it. If this was a different sort of book and I was a different sort of writer (not to mention a different sort of human being), this is the part where I'd enumerate the great lengths I took to get the scoop and how, time and again, my scrappy, one-woman operation was denied access to the labor pumping through Disney Corp's gilded innards. I'd tell you how hard I tried to get the goods, and then I'd sort of bravely make do without.

Truth is: other than the one time I sent what was, in retrospect, a super weird and slightly tipsily conceived email[48]

---

48 This email also included discursive thoughts about ekphrastic poetry and memento mori for pets. I did not hear back.

to someone I know who once mentioned that she knows someone who maybe knows-and-or-once-knew someone who was definitely at one time a high-ranking member of the show's production team, I made no effort to access any of the people whose job it is to make *The Bachelor*. The reason for that is both simple and complicated, and both sides of the coin can be summed up this way: uh, I didn't really want to.

Whether justification for a failure of reporting or a valid, critically distant MO, I'll leave to you, but either way, here's the upshot: this is about what *The Bachelor*'s production looks like, not about how the show is actually produced. Consider this the outside scoop. A couch-eye view.

And so, to employ the franchise's favorite segue, *with that being said* . . .

Because *The Bachelor*'s form has — right down to particular lines of dialogue — remained so consistent for the 16 years it has aired (as of publication), minute disturbances register with great magnitude. In the last five years, the show has made small adjustments that effect large changes to the visibility — both in manner and in degree — of its own production.

There are two things to think about when considering how the machinations behind the *Bachelor* franchise reveal themselves to us. One is how production of the show itself appears to have changed, and the other is how the world has. Remember that when *The Bachelor* debuted in 2002, the whole concept of reality TV was not only relatively new, but highly suspect. The inaugural season[49] had a slightly wheedling quality — not just explaining how the show would work, but seeming to feel the need to account for its own existence.[50] In the first episode of the show, Chris Harrison's monologue acknowledges that "trying to find love on a television show might seem a little crazy," and the first time he sits down with the Bachelor, he leads with "Alright, Alex, the most important question on everyone's mind: why on *earth* are you doing this?" With these rhetorical bones thrown to skeptics, *Bachelor* season one nosed tentatively forward, acclimatizing viewers to the idea that real, relatable folks whose true love quests might be worth rooting for could also be those who would willingly display themselves on television.

Even though the show gained quick traction as a hit, a certain defensiveness lingered, working its way down from the surface and into the joints of the machine. The argument shifted from plausibility to authenticity. Having successfully demonstrated that real people really will turn up to look for love on TV, *The Bachelor* now had to justify itself as something other real people could comfortably let themselves believe in.

But with matrimonial proof made in the *Bachelor*'s delectable pudding only rarely,[51] there was little to offer in the way

---

49 This season, by the way, is worth a rewatch for the fashion alone.

50 The first season of *The Bachelorette* faced a different burden of self-justification for the faux pas of letting a real live lady and her lady parts headline a show where she would kiss, talk to, and possibly bonk more than one human man. The show is forced to repeatedly address what it calls "the sexist double standard."

51 For a long time, Trista and Ryan Sutter were the exception in a long line of called-off engagements.

of hard evidence that the show was a means to true love. And so, in the absence of success, *The Bachelor* clung to the next best thing: dependability. Even from its first seasons, despite the fact that it had taken no runs at developing house style, the show was nonetheless predictable, even-keeled. It projected an image of something complete, ready-made, and vacuum sealed — no assembly required.

This is manifest in what, for many years, we saw of *The Bachelor*'s production. Namely: not much. It's a form of authenticity that sells itself not by its *vérité*, but by establishing an end result and then showing no trace of the weight of manufacturing behind it. This is the fantasy of a labor-free product. It's something that earns its authenticity by appearing to already exist — appearing to simply appear. The show's look was airbrushed: recognizably artificial, but thinly veiling the means that made it so.

This is not to say that the existence of the show's cameras and crew were never addressed in the early and middle years of *The Bachelor*. But these moments are few and far between, used only in the service of the highest, most mouth-watering drama. For example, the show has always been quick to pull its medical team into the frame in the service of instantly skyrocketing stakes from emotional turmoil to actual, bodily danger.[52]

So far as its status as a produced object was acknowledged

---

52 This has been a staple move from the beginning: the very first season of *The Bachelor* delivered the very first on-set panic attack. This moment featured painful, can't-look-away footage of an eliminated contestant holding her hands to the sky and pleading for "just one deep breath *please*." The show almost seemed not to know what to do with the gold turned up in its pan, letting the episode trail off awkwardly *in media res*.

in early seasons, this took place on a neatly defined set of terms, most of which were articulated by the emissary figure of Chris Harrison.[53] Through Harrison, the show carefully emphasizes the labor involved in pre-filming: the months spent "search[ing] the entire country" and "conducting a series of background checks." This projects the notion that the work of making the show is more like being importer-exporters than manufacturing: simply delivering the materials and letting them spin themselves into something that, in the absence of a visible maker, audiences might choose to regard as an inevitable expression of truth.

So, here's the thing: even as production was written out of the script on the micro level, *Bachelor* 1.0 was far easier to read for production on the macro. Just as an airbrushed image clearly telegraphs its intent to highlight and diminish, the era of *The Bachelor* and *Bachelorette* that took pains to cover up its own production also seemed far more obviously and literally scripted. Basically, the show felt more fictional. It looked super fake.

It's hard to isolate individual moments in what was really a thick saturation of tone. One thing, as I've discussed already in Chapter 3, comes up in the way certain early and middle-year villains are shown to practically drum their fingers together and cackle in their performance of something wicked this way coming. Similarly, the show also had a habit of staging elaborate set pieces around the casting of the next season's Bachelor

---

53 Harrison, incredibly, does not have a production credit on the main shows. He's in the cast but not of them.

or Bachelorette that were about as subtle as an animated, blinking arrow dropping down over the contestant's head.

On Jillian Harris's *Bachelorette* season, for example, her sixth-place suitor, Jake Pavelka, is primed for Bachelor with a drawn out dumbshow in which he crashes villain Wes's hometown date to bravely deliver news of Wes's girlfriend to Jill. In addition to being cheesily scripted and staged, this story is also, on a basic plot level, totally nonsensical: Jake claims that Wes confided to him about this girlfriend "on several occasions" while they were co-competitors and, in the same breath, alleges to have "jumped on an airplane . . . just as fast as I possibly could" upon hearing the news, despite the fact that he's been off the show for at least a week. (They've got Jake in his pilot's uniform in this scene under the vague pretense that he not only hopped on that plane, but heroically flew it himself.) As far as I can tell, no one is pretending that any of this makes sense, and yet still the show insists on a series of mannered and confusing encounters (Jill and Jake, Jake and Wes, Jake and Wes and Jill, etc.). The only function here is to crudely remind the audience that Jake is a Good Guy, no matter how flimsily reasoned or improbable the narrative used to make the point.

Next season when Jake does, indeed, become the Bachelor (surprise!), the show uses a slightly less confusing but equally artless sequence to promote Ali Fedotowsky to Bachelorette. After running out of paid time off from her job,[54] Ali sends

---

54 She worked at Facebook — a job she did ultimately leave to become Bachelorette. I really want to know if she had shares.

herself off Jake's season in the name of, you know, not losing her livelihood. After making this extremely sound decision, Ali has an alleged change of heart and, with the unexplained presence of a camera there to capture the moment, phones Jake, begging to return to the show, thus transforming her story from that of cold career woman to lovelorn reject. This, presumably, in order to reassure viewers of her *Bachelorette*-worthy heartbreak.

My point is not to invest time in debunking these story-lines — which the show barely bothers to bunk in the first place — but to point out the way the middling middle era of the show often staged choreography in an irrational, pro-duction-free vacuum. The amateur acting, loosely arranged script, and unaccountable perspective of the camera make for whole jags of seasons in which the thing the show most closely resembles, honestly, is porn. Just, you know, minus the sex.

As I've said before, *The Bachelor* has developed over time by doubling and tripling down on itself. The show has turned inward as it moves forward, growing into comfort with arch, ironic self-reference. What I want to emphasize here is that *Bachelor* 1.0 showed no such tendencies. For a fairly long time, the show did not polish its craft to reveal the height of its shine, but rather buffed it down to erase all fine-grain evidence of its production. The aesthetic that resulted was a lot like a look common to girls in high school at the time: matte, thorough pancake makeup that blotted away all evidence of zits, but left that telltale orange streak between the neck and jaw.

Before seeming too self-righteously secure in the finer tuning of our modern viewership, it's important, I think, to consider from whence *The Bachelor* comes. So, lest we forget what it felt like to bob up and down on the carousel of the aughts: I urge you to reach back for a moment. Picture: Michael Moore at the Oscar podium in 2003, gadfly and flyover prophet standing in the entertainment industry's coastal epicenter to call out our existence under fictitious political premises, our lives lived in fictitious times. Now think of 2005: Stephen Colbert — in the early days of what would be more than a decade of living in public as a fictional character — defining "truthiness" for the benefit of *The Colbert Report* pilot. In 2006, Merriam-Webster would declare it the word of the year.

I offer these tidbits in the hopes that one will dissolve on your palate like a madeleine. Because I think as we look back on *The Bachelor*, it's a useful exercise to try not only to remember, but to really recall — if I may be so bold as to urge you to really, bodily *feel* — the sheer gravitational pressure that weighed on the border between fiction and nonfiction in the era of the show's development. And, in particular, to envision the way that border seemed to waver and flicker and dissolve when we tried to capture it, as we so often did, on TV and in movies. From here and now, it may seem like fuss made over the placement of a sapling in what we know to be a thriving, multinational forest. But at the time, a basic question about what reality was and where we might look for it — or more accurately *watch* it — was charged with profound, potentially shattering uncertainty about who we were and what representative technologies might lead us to become.

This is not to suggest that such questions and their attendant anxieties have since been eradicated — in fact, they've gone from presence to omnipresence. But what's important to remember is how at the time, a large proportion of energetic angst was focused on cultural products, of which there was a more limited range. That is to say, it felt very, very important that we not mistake real for fake onscreen. The very terms on which these questions are premised (real, fake, screen) have since been extracted and filtered through so many prismatic generations of devices — each of which is physically smaller and more widely available than the last — that I think it's difficult to reverse-engineer the initial burst of light by memory alone. Or maybe I really mean more like the opposite: that the unfiltered version of these fears exists *only* in acts of nostalgic recall.

Either way, if we're going to really crack open *The Bachelor*, I think we have to try to roll something back in our minds and our feels. Because if, for the better part of a decade, American life was boggled and transfixed by a seemingly simple ontological riddle, then the proliferation of shows like *The Bachelor* were both the resulting cluster headache and the best analgesic on the market. And even as our nervous systems lit up with anxiety over what might emerge from the unholy mating of "reality" and "television," still so many of us giddily, guiltily flicked on the tube.

So once upon a time, *The Bachelor* glossed over its production, and yet still it came across as highly artificially produced. I don't think the contradiction is only a testament to what rubes we viewers were only a short decade ago. That's an interpretation I find tempting, but incomplete. I'll suggest instead that what *The Bachelor* packaged and sold was never intended to pass for unalloyed reality. It was rather working its way towards an authenticity defined not by results, but by the degree to which it answered to viewers' authentically felt needs: a bundle of desires that could no longer be mollified with either well-wrought artistic visions or sturdily rendered facts. Set in fictitious times, at the dawning age of truthiness, *The Bachelor* was a respite from the exhausting responsibility of segregating truth and fiction altogether.

Scrubbing itself of minor evidence of its manufacturing gave the show cover not to bother hiding the broad strokes of its artifice. It also gave viewers cover to stop giving a shit about what was or wasn't real. This lower-order authenticity was only ever meant to shelter us with plausible deniability, not to pass a more robust stress test for belief. So if the results now read crude and fake to a contemporary viewer, that's not necessarily — or at least not *only* — because we have evolved better bullshit detectors. It's because we now ask for different kinds of entertainment to transport us from a different kind of world.

The first-gen version of *The Bachelor* and *Bachelorette* was a Wonka-esque confection — something that might delude you with the sensation of a turkey dinner poured down your throat as you smacked thoughtlessly on a stick of low-cal gum. It was submission to familiarity in a foreign, unregulated form, producing all the pleasure of the soapiest fictions accompanied by all the satisfaction of real-life outcomes: relationships that could be followed offscreen, tracked by the surveillance of tabloid news and the internet into the world at large where, generally, they would go to die.

Then something changed. And, like most changes that matter, it happened by way of small, erratic, mostly unplanned movements, the sum of which have made for a seismic shift.

A few memorable fissures in the well-wrought romance terrarium:

In 2012, it came out that one of the front-running suitors on Emily Maynard's season of *The Bachelorette*, race car driver Arie Luyendyk Jr.,[55] had dated a producer years prior to filming. Though this was apparently not intended for inclusion in the arc of the show, the world off camera intervened, and gossip sleuthed out and circulated during the show's airing forced a late-stage edit to accommodate the would-be-untold storyline. And so it is that in episode seven, in the middle of a one-on-one date between Emily and Arie in Prague, the narrative jolts, and we swing back to California, where, from the steps of the *Bachelor* mansion, Chris Harrison addresses "something you may have heard — or even read about." He names producer Cassie Lambert, admits to her many-years-old history with Arie, and explains that Emily herself learned the story only well into filming. From there, "in the interest

---

55 Who is improbably being resurrected as the Bachelor 2018.

of full disclosure," Harrison segues into an unorthodox ITM between Cassie and Emily that is totally, remarkably un-*Bachelor*.

The clip opens on Cassie Lambert's back, her split ends peeking over the lip of her leather jacket as she adjusts Emily's microphone to the tune of the unfiltered shuffle of mic on fabric. When Cassie turns around and heads to her place offscreen, we are delivered something brief and glorious: a glimpse of the unsmiling, focused, neutrally made-up face[56] of a woman at work. Someone doing her job.

For the next two minutes of unscored footage that look (or are made to look) like scraps freshly salvaged off the cutting room floor, Emily is the most animate she appears all season. In the cadence of friend-talk rather than the mannered con-figurations of sound bite we are accustomed to, Emily speaks from a perspective the show has never before let us in on: what it feels like to be making *The Bachelorette* rather than *being* the Bachelorette. Emily makes the kinds of casual, inside-baseball references that would normally never make it to air, glancing around as she refers to "everyone" making the show, calling Cassie "my producer," speaking to offscreen relationships like Cassie's engagement to "Pete." Rather than send Chris Harrison to pop up like a cartoon paperclip to explain the ref-erence to executive producer Peter Scalettar, the show leaves all of this as is, letting Emily's articulation of her surroundings

---

56 This flicker is all the more human and disruptive appearing as it does in the frame with Emily Maynard, who is accurately and precisely gorgeous, but also manages to project still-ness even when she is in motion. There is a high real-doll quotient to her beauty, even for a Bachelorette.

reveal that the production normally left out of view is not a machine, but a series of relationships — a community.

The actual content of what Emily says also convincingly humanizes both the Bachelorette and the production. Basically, she's (rightfully, imho) pissed to have been left out of the loop not because she's threated by Arie and Cassie's ancient history, but because it exposes Arie's collusion with the show's incomplete truths. Emily asks Cassie, "If he's okay with hiding that he even knows you, much less dated you, and we've been hanging out for so long, like, what the fuck else is he hidin', you know? He's a good actor." As Cassie explains her own rationale in delaying disclosure and tries to account for Arie's having shared in the silence, Emily pushes back, describing ways Arie might have behaved more like a person than an ascending reality TV star.

And then Emily Maynard says something completely amazing that, I argue, quietly and permanently revolutionized the *Bachelor* franchise: "This isn't like a production thing — it's like a *real-life* thing. You know? This isn't, like, for the show." And just in case we missed it, she says it again a moment later with slightly different emphasis: "It's not a production thing — it's like a real-life *thing*."

Emily has been made to feel foolish by the conflation of these categories — real life and production — and is trying to re-establish the boundary between them. When Emily says "it," she means something like: the situation, her frustration, her hurt feelings. But by airing this moment with a gloss-free glory that purports to bare itself completely, the show manages to brilliantly insinuate that "it" is the show itself. The very fact of showing this footage in the spirit of "full disclosure" performs a jiujitsu move with the weight of Emily's words, redirecting her attack to serve in the show's defense.

The moments selected from Emily and Cassie's exchange (though limitedly edited, these are nonetheless selections) are telling. They appear calculated to be maximally raw. What results is not only an unprecedented admission to the existence of production, but a statement about its quality: these two minutes insist that the show is not only a product of labor, but a labor of love. And there in the thick of it, we get word from the star of the show herself: this isn't a production thing — it's a *real-life* thing. It's a real-life *thing*.

In 2014, Andi Dorfman's season of *The Bachelorette* faced an ethical issue on real-life vs. production turf when one of its contestants, Eric Hill, was killed in a paragliding accident very shortly after his exit from the show, while the final episodes were still being shot. To make things more complicated, Hill was an early front-runner who also had an early flameout by committing the *Bachelor* sin of questioning where real life ended and production began, telling the Bachelorette that he saw "two different sides of Andi," and that "little glimpses of you, like the real you . . . that's the Andi I like." In a heart-to-heart gone awry, Eric secures his exit when he declares, "I came on this to meet a person, not a TV actress."

Even had Hill not died, this confrontation alone leads to

an unveiling of the conditions of the show's production. "Do you feel like you've been comfortable and natural the whole time?" Eric asks Andi. Her response:

> Am I comfortable and natural all the time? Not a chance. But do I work my ass off and stay up late so that everyone knows that I am here for them — yeah, I do. You have no idea what it takes. You have no idea how exhausted I am. You have no clue how it is to look people in the face and send them home. You have no idea . . . That is the one thing: I have come into this and tried to be natural . . . Do I not realize that there's cameras everywhere? Do I not realize there's guys right there? [*looks around, gestures at production out-of-frame*] Yes, I do. But you're seriously still insulting me.

This is one of those rare moments when, as with Emily Maynard's interview, we get the lead's take on not just occupying the role, but making the show. While Bachelors and Bachelorettes often speak to the emotional toll of hurting people's feelings, it's rare to hear someone address labor conditions and the physical demands of the show's long hours. Andi continues in this vein when she addresses the remaining men moments later, telling them through frustrated, half-yelling tears: "I have done nothing but try to be natural for y'all. This is not easy for me. I am exhausted. I am so exhausted. And I am trying so hard, I really am . . . This is so real to me. Every single day this is real to me."

Here's what's so interesting about this: what sends Andi over the edge emotionally, twanging on her last unslept nerve, is Eric's suggestion that she's an actress — someone hired to inhabit and perform a fiction, to pretend something that isn't real. In fact, Andi *has* been hired — only unlike an actress, her job isn't to perform a truth, but to live it. Not to pretend, but to be. In these speeches, Andi reveals that she has to work unnaturally hard to be natural. Which makes sense: with the cameras, crew, lights, producers, and sets, ABC already has all the trappings of television. The Bachelorette is hired to deliver the reality. Eric's interpretation is so wounding to Andi because she really is doing a job, and it's much harder than the one he's accused her of. The Bachelorette's labor isn't acting — it's falling in love.

This season of *The Bachelorette* opened with a dedication to Hill, and following his exit in episode four, the rose ceremony is cut from the edit and replaced with a conversation between Chris Harrison and Andi about the impact of Hill's presence on the show. In episode eight, we are there in the room when, just after her last hometown date, Andi and her final four suitors are gathered in Chris Harrison's L.A. living room as the host delivers news of Hill's death.

After a few minutes of filming the stars' reactions in the usual *Bachelor* manner, there is a literal, physical shift. The camera continues rolling but makes a 180° turn to face producers, dips, shows a view of the ground, and is eventually propped on a tripod in the corner. From this vantage, we watch the cast and crew mingle in their grief. We hear textures of fabric on mic packs as many long hugs are exchanged. A producer holds the Bachelorette and whispers consolations. "I don't know if I can do it, Alicia," Andi whisper-sobs. And we're there, watching, for all of it. For a moment, it's not that production has broken through and left its trace on the show's narrative: the interaction between production and real life has *become* the show.

As it graduated into the mid-teens, *The Bachelor*'s collisions with the world outside its universe increasingly provoked the show to expose elements of its own making onscreen. As a result of moments like the ones on Emily's season and Andi's, since 2012 there has been a general easing of the boundary between production and product. We've arrived at a place where it's become relatively common — no moment of high drama required — to see the word "producer" appear at the bottom of the screen in white, tagging and captioning the dialogue of those disembodied voices we hear from more and more.

At the same time, *The Bachelor* has dealt with increased exposure on increasingly present forms of social media. Rather than resist the proliferation of quality-uncontrolled content as a threat to the seal of its universe,[57] the show has by and large opted to embrace the unspecified, unregulated, but powerful

---

57 In spite of what I imagine must be pretty complex non-disclosure agreements, there is always the risk of plain old human error. Kaitlyn Bristowe, for example, accidentally spoiled her season when she Snapchatted a candid shot lying in bed with winner Shawn Booth halfway through the season's airing. She meant to send the snap to a producer (producers and stars: they're really friends!) but flipped it to her followers instead.

marketing potential of its social media appeal. And while *The Bachelor* was becoming a kind of Instagram-fame generator for its participants, producers' stars also rose.

In 2013, in an incident that did not directly touch the *Bachelor*'s onscreen life but nonetheless reverberated there, a volley of tweets from franchise producer Elan Gale went viral. It was American Thanksgiving weekend, and from within the gnarly, all-too-human density of the country's most heinous day of travel, Gale sent out a tweet calling out the rude behavior of an entitled fellow passenger. After boarding the plane, Gale continued to document and live-tweet first his attempts to quell the offender (one Diane in seat 7A) with drinks and passive-aggressive notes, and then a series of increasingly agitated responses from his on-board nemesis. The incident ends with *Bachelor*-worthy drama: Diane slaps Elan in the face upon landing. Someone call the on-set medics.

This incident was, I kid you not, reported all over the world. It drew attention for a number of reasons: for one thing, it must have been a slow news day, but also, for so many Americans boxed in transit with their own Dianes, Gale's tweetstorm was the revenge fantasy we didn't know we'd been waiting for. It was cathartic. And there was something compelling but uncomfortable in the way the dynamics of the story's power veered as things escalated and Gale graduated from sarcasm and wine delivery to the imperative that Diane "suck [his] dick." Once elicited, our pity and fear no longer had a clear place to land as Gale went from minor Airbus hero to questionable vigilante in a few short, 140-character paces.

Always ready for a good doxxing, the internet jumped in to ID Diane. Someone claimed her as a relative and revealed she was a terminal cancer patient. Everyone was right and everyone was wrong and the whole murky affair seemed like it might be a model or a warning — might tell us something about the effect of social media on private decency and public shame.

And if the story was well made, that seemed in no small part due to Gale's skills as a producer: that ability to take the messiness of an experience lived in real time and recast it with narrative verve. But then a few days later, Gale revealed the whole thing to have been a hoax: a no-harm-no-foul fiction conjured to entertain himself and his Twitter followers through the dull stress of holiday travel. His story may have spoken to the real needs and questions of the moment, but it was never actually real. At the time, Gale had 35,000 Twitter followers. On the day I am writing this, he has 200,000. That's partly a function of more people using Twitter in general, but it's also a reflection of Gale's increased fame.

By Kaitlyn Bristowe's season of *The Bachelorette* in 2015, when a contestant got into an altercation with production in his exit interview and the camera panned past Kaitlyn's shoulder to look out on the driveway of the *Bachelor* mansion, many plugged-in viewers would know the agitated cloud of hair in the standoff as Gale. For a good portion of the show's devoted, 'gramming-and-tweeting viewership, this view would not represent a tear in the fabric of *The Bachelor*'s fantasy, but an access point to drop deeper into its layers. Witnessing Gale at work — even better, to see him pulled into the narrative by way of threat to physical safety — only enriches the spectrum of *Bachelor* technicolor. It's more celebrity sighting than glimpse of the fallen, fragile wizard behind the curtain.

There *is* one recent point of access to the show's innards that the franchise has neither licensed nor embraced. Launched on Lifetime in 2015, *UnREAL* is a scripted TV show about the production of a (fictional) reality show called *Everlasting*: a competitive dating show in which women live together in a mansion while pursuing an eligible "suitor." *UnREAL*'s co-creator, Sarah Gertrude Shapiro, has cred as a producer on the *Bachelor* franchise.

Shapiro's fictional avatar is Rachel Goldberg: an *Everlasting* producer with a unique gift for manipulating those around her, both on the show and off it. *UnREAL* is about Rachel's antiheroic struggle to determine if her professional talent destines her for post-*Everlasting* greatness or if, as her psychiatrist mother would have her believe, her gifts are symptomatic of a longstanding mental illness with a roving diagnosis somewhere between borderline and antisocial personality disorder. Which doesn't seem so unlikely given the heinous shit Rachel does so well at her job. The producers of *Everlasting* cast women in roles like "wifey," "evil bitch," and "desperate MILF" and then do whatever it takes to bring those characters to life — from befriending and backstabbing contestants to more, if you will, *dramatic* measures like withholding medication and shipping in abusive ex-husbands for drop-by visits.

There are big differences between *The Bachelor* and the faux-show *Everlasting* that keep *UnREAL* from being read as a how-to blueprint.[58] Insofar as *UnREAL* is a portrait of *The Bachelor*, the reflection is spiritual, not literal. *UnREAL* also makes a point of deviating from the *Bachelor* universe in ways that highlight the franchise's failures. While it's a takeoff of a show in which women interact with one another *exclusively* to discuss a man, *UnREAL*'s first season[59] was a Bechdel Test–crusher. Similarly, in the second season, Rachel's big professional success comes from achieving a longstanding goal to cast "the first Black suitor," needling at *The Bachelor*'s own notoriously retrograde record on race. The second season of *UnREAL* aired in 2016, and the following year, life would (finally) imitate fiction, with the real *Bachelor* franchise casting a Black lead for the first time with Rachel Lindsay as Bachelorette.[60]

If nothing else, *UnREAL* has proved that *The Bachelor* is a richer, more bounteous resource of good content than the show itself would care to admit, and even its spindly, wayward estuaries are ones many of us are happy to follow. I guess when your claim to fame is that you're the most dramatic ever, there's enough drama to go around.

Not everyone feels this way. The only unofficial official word from the *Bachelor* franchise on the subject of their

---

58 *Everlasting*, for example, is improbably broadcast in real time. Which makes for better fictional plots (the irreversible mistakes!) than dramatizing the slow burn of *Bachelor* editing would.

59 After a smart, jagged, delectable first season, the show pretty much devolves into sad narrative sludge.

60 More on this in Chapter 7.

scripted impersonator comes (of course) from Chris Harrison, who has accused the show of being a weak hanger-on to *The Bachelor*'s coattails, calling the results "really terrible."[61] Harrison has also made a point of jabbing at *UnREAL*'s relatively low ratings: the premiere of the second season took in about a tenth of the audience as did episode one of that year's *Bachelor*. Which is like saying that more people watch the Super Bowl than the Puppy Bowl. Duh. That doesn't mean people don't like puppies.

In terms of popularity, *UnREAL* is the opposite of *The Bachelor*, which is a show everyone seems to watch, but no one wants to be seen taking seriously. *UnREAL* is one of those classic meh-rated shows that, at least in its first season, scored a lot of positive critical attention.[62] Not quite a critical darling, but definitely a show critics have gotten a good flirt on with. Let's put it this way: *UnREAL* might not get the final rose, but it would totally make it to fantasy suites.

I've been talking, generally speaking, about the way tidal shifts in culture have registered in how we see *The Bachelor*'s production. It's worth emphasizing that the kinds of broad social changes I'm talking about are felt on multiple dimensions that

---

61 Later, once *UnREAL* had been picked up for a second season, Harrison would not quite recant this statement, but would change tack, saying he doesn't bother to watch the show at all: he just chanced to channel-surf upon it one time and caught a glimpse of something he thought was weak.

62 It won the Critics' Choice Television Award for Most Exciting New Series in 2015, plus a Peabody, and was nominated for an Emmy for writing.

directly impact the show's making: producers (human beings), consumers (human beings), and the primary material from which the show's narrative is extracted (also: human beings).

Like most reality TV shows, one of *The Bachelor*'s central strategies for making stories happen is to cut contestants off as much as possible from experiences of interiority. The two-pronged approach of forbidding contestants' access to recording technology while dousing the *Bachelor* mansion with disinhibiting substances[63] diverts contestants' inner-monologues, chasing every thought and feeling to the surface so it may be captured, recorded, and (re-)told. To this end, it would seem to be a huge benefit to the task of producing the show that, in general, a taste for exposing one's inner life in public has risen (or fallen, depending on your perspective) to meet *The Bachelor* where it always already was.

In an oral history of the show for *The Cut* in 2016, executive producer Mike Fleiss says that this shift in contestants' demeanors, from camera-shy to duck-faced,[64] represents the biggest change in making the show. Here's what's interesting: Fleiss articulates this as a movement from artifice to authenticity, exactly inverting the generically anti-Millennial line you might have gotten used to hearing from those of a certain age, wealth, and position of power. Rather than bemoaning the cagey superficiality of the youths, Fleiss believes that contemporary *Bachelor* contestants' worn-in, comfy self-images allow

---

63 Just alcohol so far as I know, but also whatever chemicals the body produces from insufficient sleep.

64 My words, not his.

them to project onscreen personae that more closely resemble their actual selves.

Obviously Fleiss has a vested interest in imagining the show on an upward trajectory, but still I find the totality of the reversal at work here to be surprising. With no trace of nostalgia for the dignity of self-preservation, Fleiss remembers the first *Bachelor* initiates as "so guarded" and "afraid of everything." He recalls a three-hour-long ordeal to get one woman out of a robe and into a hot tub, comparing this to today's contestants who "dive right in."

In some ways, that willingness to jump in the pool offers a kind of easing on all fronts: producers are given more malleable material from which to work, and participants are empowered to be more astute, active participants in their own production. Everyone, as Mike Fleiss seems to want to suggest, has gotten a little bit better at being who they're supposed to be.

But where each role begins and ends has also loosened. And as much as being raised with disciplined training in confession empowers reality TV participants in some ways, it also makes them vulnerable in others. Contemporary *Bachelor* and *Bachelorette* contestants may be accustomed to living with a higher level of exposure, but they are also used to having access to a wide variety of means through which to download and process their emotional lives. That is to say: today's contestants may turn up at the *Bachelor* mansion more media-ready, but they're also going cold turkey on the ability to mediate their lives. And though we're fond of conflating these sorts of things, just because someone's selfie game is on point, it doesn't mean they're any better equipped to live without their support system, their habits, their distractions: in short, to live without the trappings of real life.

To the extent that current *Bachelor* contestants have prior experience onscreen, a lot of that comes by way of holding the (phone) camera themselves. Their DIY skills are as much in controlling, filtering, and editing — that is *producing* — their lives as in performing them. Likewise, producers are becoming more and more visible on the *Bachelor* screen, growing into recurring roles on the show. Surrounding, reflecting, and watching all of this, viewers are invited to get their jollies by projecting themselves with imaginative sympathy into *either* role.

As the barriers and responsibilities between its producers, consumers, and means of production have appeared to thin, *The Bachelor* has outgrown the image of hermetic completeness it once projected. And as it's moved away from those origins as a spectacle that made labor invisible, the show has grown into a new fantasy — one that, rather that erasing labor, neutralizes it through alleged exposure. Allowing us to see its seams selectively, *The Bachelor* secures a modern form of authenticity, implying that its capacity for revelation is, as Fleiss imagines contestants' to be, authentic and total. Under the influence of a new kind of naturalism, the show invites viewers to strip down to our own bikinis, hop into a narrative whirlpool just warm enough to be a melting pot. Don't be afraid — the water is warm. Dunk under. Immerse yourself. Come out new.

5

Bachelor Nation: Viewers

It's Monday night in America. The house is warm and the lights are turned up — even the room with the TV on is brightly lit. This is not a time to sit quietly in the dark: everyone wants to see their score sheets, their drinks. They want to be able to see one another. There are too many people for the couch, of course, but no one minds — the carpet is soft. Does everyone have enough snacks? Don't worry, there's plenty more in the kitchen. Glasses of wine are topped all the way up. Everyone drinks at "journey" and "amazing," drinks to every kiss.

There's a knock at the door.

After a few lean years through the middle, *The Bachelor* has had a comeback, securing mostly steady or rising ratings since about 2012. More impressive than the number of viewers,[65] though, is the remarkable fact that the show has acquired coveted, ad-baiting demos, performing well both against itself and against competitors with adults ages 18 to 34, households with six-figure-plus incomes, and women. *The Bachelor*'s numbers are good by any standard, but fantastic for a show of its age. In 2017, Nick Viall's season of *The Bachelor* was the *only* show on network television to grow its audience from the year before. It also cleans up in auxiliary categories like tweets per timeslot, by which Nielsen attempts to capture a show's influence on what industry insiders call simply "social" (no "media" required on this journey to find nominalization).

But the most interesting thing about *Bachelor* viewership is hard to capture even with that concession to "social" success. Traditional ratings tally screens, not viewers, and Bachelor Nation (as the show has dubbed its audience) is known for rallying groups around a single set for viewing parties. The show leans into this unique feature of its viewership when it sends Chris Harrison out to deliver the annual state of the union, reminding us of who we are: "Bachelor Nation, you guys watch the show unlike any other group of fans: you watch it together."

Each season, Harrison and the Bachelor take to the nation's streets to perform a ritual of crashing a lucky few

---

65 As soon as you reach more than a couple of years back, total number of viewers are a misleading metric not only for *The Bachelor*, but for all TV shows. The sheer volume of available programming now as compared to the era in which *The Bachelor* debuted has eroded total numbers of viewers for all shows, across the board. For example, the all-time most-watched episode of *The Bachelor* was the finale of season two, which took in 25.9 million viewers as compared to season 20's finale, which was watched by 9.5 million.

fans' viewing parties with cameras in tow, broadcasting the *Bachelor*-maniacal results at the "Women Tell All" live show. "Season in, season out, this never gets old. This is like fuel," Harrison says, flattering us, I guess, with a concession to the vampirism of celebrity.

The remarkable thing about the *Bachelor* viewing party is that it reveals how, alongside all the many tropes of its semifictional universe, *The Bachelor* has also successfully manufactured archetypes for its consumption. These on-air windows of access into Bachelor Nation's heartland make its constitution clear: thou shalt gather in detached, carpeted homes, in multigenerational, matriarchal congregations at least ten women strong, be wine-buzzed, etc. Every season, Harrison ends the montage by aiming his piercing baby blues at the camera (and into my soul) to say, "Bachelor Nation, we love you so much."

The Bachelor has a funny way of both tapping and training viewers' desires. In doing so, it once again reveals an incredible ability to double down on its now-ancient origins and still feel contemporary. At a moment when it's permissible — almost to the point of default — to watch TV while spooning your laptop in a nest of solitude, queuing episode after episode in surrender to a particular kind of self-loathing pleasure, *The Bachelor* refuses this paradigm altogether. It's the opposite of a binge watch: insistently episodic, locked into the pocket of its Monday night airing, churning at a serial slow-roll. The show itself may go spelunking in the depths of human loneliness, but its viewers can never be lonely: they are engaged social citizens. *The Bachelor* is a standing date, an event — not a product to be consumed, but an experience to be had. It's a reason to celebrate. The life of the viewing party.

Just how common is that *Bachelor* viewing party phenomenon, really? Thing is, it totally doesn't matter. The viewing party is highly serviceable as a piece of propaganda because it seems intuitively right, but can only be proven in anecdotal glimpses. What's more, by endorsing the watching of the show as a well-attended social occasion, *The Bachelor* severs its currency from Nielsen's gold standard. Even if *Bachelor* ratings are good — and often great — the viewing party narrative insists that no matter what the numbers show, the truth is always something bigger, better, and unaccounted for. Around every *Bachelor*-tuned screen, there's a packed house, a whole party. A nation on watch.

But wait! This would not be *Bachelor* logic without one more brilliant and contradictory twist: *The Bachelor* insists on the value of something old fashioned, but it's definitely not analog. Rather, the show taps nostalgia for IRL social experience while still forming a deep, devilish bond with social media, which, like any good satanic contract, has enabled the show to grow younger with time. A 2015 analysis of the show's performance in the trade magazine *Ad Age* suggests that the show's early and committed adoption of hashtags, live-tweets, and fantasy leagues is the source of its late-life resurgence, its ageless golden age.

The Bachelor has recast itself as something not to be consumed, but responded to: a call to which we, the people, must answer. And so *The Bachelor* holds itself above and beyond ratings in two fantastically opposed ways. The viewing party story casts the show as a priceless curio, a form of civic bonding as invaluable as an ice cream social. At the same time, the show's robust second life online reassures any viewer not wolf-packed around a communal screen that the real party is one you can log on to — it's happening wherever you already are.

It's a particularly modern kind of manipulation: to be both the condition of FOMO and the promise of its cure. And in this, *The Bachelor* has yoked itself to the cultural power of social media more broadly: that ability to be democratic, ubiquitous, and yet still create an impression of rarified value. As an analogy, think for a moment of the status of social media companies themselves, many of which have nine- and ten-figure valuations without having ever turned a profit. If we give any credence to the invisible hand's signals, it would seem we recognize the power of masses of human beings providing evidence of themselves, even if we haven't yet figured out how to harness that energy and put it to use. We may not know what to do with it, but we know it's there.

Similarly, *The Bachelor* tells us the story of a value that lies beyond the scope of traditional measures of influence. It whispers to us that it is both too pure to be measured and too cool to try — as earnest as patriotism, and as slippery as an avatar. While it slurps up ad revenue, still *The Bachelor* tells us that its influence can't be measured; it's something you just have to *feel*.

Bachelor Nation is invited to tweet their little hearts out and leave a candle burning at the viewing party window in case of crashers, but the one time the franchise tried to build a more direct pipeline from couch to screen, things didn't go so hot. In its fateful final season, *Bachelor Pad* further gummed up its web of gimmicks with a twofer of drama and fan service, casting a handful of *Bachelor* viewers alongside the traditional mainstage rejects. "This is just magic," one fan-turned-cast-member gushes at the threshold of the *Pad*, "I've seen this house on TV, and Chris Harrison knows my name."

With their hopeful, studied crushes and trigger-happy selfie urges, the fans screeched into the mansion like a pack of horny bonobos sent to dilute a captive population's gene pool. And as sometime happens in a kingdom governed by primal instincts, the *Bachelor* pack caught a whiff of the foreign scent, closed ranks, and left the outsiders to feed on scraps as they picked them off one by one.

It was truly remarkable: a group of people who had moments before been busy reviewing their network of intractable hatreds now quickly unified by the perceived entitlement of nativism. As contestant Rachel griped: "You didn't earn your spot here. You didn't get dumped on national television yet." Another, Jaclyn, was more speculative: "They're going to sniff our underwear! They're so creepy. Don't even let them come in." In a swift, feudal movement, the house was divided between an underclass of fame-grubbers and elites empowered by willful amnesia, forgetting that they, too, had only lately washed up the

Bachelor mansion's driveway hungry for something elusive. You might even say: looking for a better life.

The *Bachelor* logic vis-à-vis suffering and its redemptive gifts proved more powerful than anything else: not only empathy, but also self-serving motivations like strategy or sexual attraction that might have moved alums to admit the Bachelor Nationals. The driving force of the *Bachelor*'s machine prevailed, quashing any good drama that might have been milked out of the crossbreeding between Bachelor Nation and Bachelor Family — commoners and royals. The *Pad* was an unbreachable caste system, and the experiment in VIP fan service more or less a failure.

In the spirit of the show's own inclination to conflate what a person feels with what is true, I'm going to go ahead and say that in the last few seasons, *The Bachelor* has come to seem like something everyone[66] watches. This popularity feels like weather, like ambience: the fluttering of a million little tweets. It's come by way of a quantity and quality combo. Without ever missing a beat as a tabloid staple, the show has been taken up by more prestige media, put through the thinkpiece wringer, and still, amazingly, come out the other side without

---

66 Just a sampling of some of the well-known among the everyones: public intellectual Roxane Gay watches and writes about the show, actress Anna Kendrick has one of the best *Bachelor* live-tweeting habits in the game, and comedian Amy Schumer is a fan (she also had a heroic appearance on Kaitlyn's season). Even Kareem Abdul-Jabbar, one of the greatest professional basketball players of all time, once wrote a scathing, eloquent, and revealingly *Bachelor*-familiar critique of the show's racial dynamics (leading him, too, to take on a guest appearance). I could go on and on.

having been stripped of its ability to be enjoyed. And somewhere along the way, as it weathered exposure, *The Bachelor* ditched the "guilty" leaching off its pleasure.

This is all quite new. It remains to be seen what it will mean that a class of young, over-educated, and ostensibly woke Americans now feel licensed to show off Bachelor Nation passports in their social media feeds. Will we slough off the know-it-all of cultural elites and freely, publicly indulge the lower orders of our taste? Or will exposure to the hyperverbal, vigilant twittering of a new demographic give *The Bachelor* cause to sand down the more pointed edges of its conservatism? (Follow-up question: exactly how much politically correct modification could the show take before it keels over and dies from a tragic lack of fun?) Is this the part where we stop pretending that we're better than the trash we love, or is it the part where, for love of country, we demand that our leaders reimagine our trashy nation as something a bit better?

Whatever the future may bring, be sure to leave your doors unlocked, Bachelor Nation. You never know when it may be time to stand up and be counted, to show your face onscreen. You never know when the mettle of your civic hospitality may be called upon. Any given Monday, you may find a Bachelor and a host — a hero and a sovereign — wandering the night, in want of shelter, just looking to feel the love.

6

Almost Paradise: Spinoffs

As it entered the twenty-teens, *The Bachelor* and *Bachelorette* faced some issues of resource management that wanted tending. As of Jason and Molly's wedding in February 2010, the show had been on the air for eight years, rolled through going-on 18 seasons, and delivered all of two love-to-marriage matches. There's no standardized metric for tallying *Bach* stats, but if you measure utterances of "I do" against the literal hundreds of rejections and breakups produced in the service of those marriages, the show was clocking a success rate of around 0.0045%. So there was that. More pressing, though, was a more ephemeral question: whither the 450-some-odd souls the show had invested in publicly, compellingly devastating?

As it turned out, the *Bachelor's* lovelorn were stumbling out of the breakupmobile and into one another's arms. The show's on-air love match rates might have been low, but as a post-production dating-slash-hookup pool, the franchise was slaying. Doing god's work, you might say.

Re: the high ratio of *Bachelor* affiliated hook-ups, I'm guessing that dating someone under reality TV surveillance and subsequently getting dumped for entertainment value is one of those things you have to have lived through to get — that it's a once-removed bonding experience for even those who have endured it separately. It also seems to me that the *Bachelor* casting process functions as an aggregator of the like-minded and the look-alike, making for a dating pool of individuals likely to recognize themselves in one another. Isn't that more or less what finding love is?

Whatever the cause, by the show's middle age, the activity of its alumni network was one to rival even the most identity-gripping, self-congratulatory of Ivy Leagues. By way of both official and unofficial reunions, cruises, and parties, the badge of being a *Bachelor* or *Bachelorette* reject was a passport to a robust IRL social network of the nearly and sometimes famous.

For the franchise, this meant not only that their love machine was not getting full credit, but also that the people they had turned into characters were falling in and out of love and bed with one another — i.e., providing dramatic content — for the benefit of no one but themselves. It must have seemed a tragic waste: hundreds of audience-tested, single, ready-to-mingle-on-camera hotties getting it on with no one watching.

Enter *Bachelor Pad*. Launched in 2010 as part of the network's summer lineup, the show promised to be the foam skimmed off *The Bachelor*'s and *Bachelorette*'s heady pour (or maybe more like the sludge skimmed out of the mansion pool post-filming, I dunno). As Chris Harrison put it in one promo for the show, for all the men and women who leave the show loveless and in tears, "There's a special place that they can go." *Bachelor Pad* brought together a batch of franchise alumni for a live-in competitive entanglement with the promise of a shot at $250,000 and a side of romance.

And if the *Bachelor* is defined by the abiding conflict between romance and game show, *Bachelor Pad*'s MO was to keep, like, ten percent of the former while tossing every trope of the latter into a Vitamix. The result was an unholy mixture of dating game, feats of strength, battle of the sexes, talent show, leadership exercise, election campaign, gamble, ethical conundrum, etc.

As briefly as possible, the basic elements: an equal-gender spread of one-time *Bachelor* and *Bachelorette* contestants bunking up in the franchise's signature mansion; the making and breaking of couples-slash-teammates forged with varying degrees of romantic attachment and competitive pragmatism; weekly competitions (a mixture of solo and doubles) demanding no particular or cohesive skill set; winners selecting participants for mini group dates accompanied by a break-off one-on-one date and immunity rose; weekly eliminations in which men vote off women and vice versa; and private voting booths followed by occasional public acts of tie-breaking.

When eight men and women are left, they are locked down in their couples (no more swaps) to perform a dance challenge because *Dancing with the Stars* tie-in, or a Cirque du Soleil challenge because publicity agreement, or a singing challenge because unclear. One couple belts, bends, or cha-chas arhythmically out of the competition while the winning team selects another pair with whom they will "compete" in the finale: a live event in which previously eliminated contestants up-vote a pair of winners based on whatsoever criteria they choose. Then, in a final turn of the screw, the winning couple is presented with a prisoner's dilemma choice of whether to share or keep a $250,000 prize: if each chooses share, they split the prize in half; if one chooses keep, that person takes it all; and if both try to keep, the prize money is divided between all other contestants.

A truly remarkable feat of syncretism, *Bachelor Pad* may be summarized, but it can never truly be explained. The fussy, weird format was neither here nor there: the *Pad* provided time with characters we'd already been trained to love, hate, and, most importantly, watch. The appeal was less about *what* and more about *who* and, to the extent that the show maintained loose adherence to its matchmaking roots, *with whom*. And despite being based on confounding, contradictory, and changing premises, *Bachelor Pad* is a show you can give yourself over to — for whole episodes, whole seasons — and experience neither the logistical confusion nor the existential crisis its corridors to nowhere ought to provoke. It is surprisingly easy to simply let it wash over you without feeling the urge to source rhyme or reason.

But, of course, as soon as you prod even a little bit — even through the basic act of description — it's pretty clear that *Bachelor Pad* makes no goddamn sense. Not because its rules can't be followed (in fact, some of the dimmer stars in the *Bachelor* sky have competed), but because it is fundamentally without purpose. The sheer number of game show tropes *Bachelor Pad* piles on creates the impression that the show itself must be a game: something that may be won or lost by virtue of one's choices, with contestants maneuvering their way to the tune of a cool quarter mill. But the show's many, and changing, and conflicting goals — to connect with a teammate, to fall in love, to win challenges, to secure allies, to beat everyone, etc. — are mutually neutralizing. For an individual competitor, every perceived step on one would-be strategic course delivers an equal blowback on some other.

Bachelor Pad was a bright hologram of a wide-open playing field projected onto The Abyss, masking profound incoherence and meaninglessness with a shiny illusion of competition. The show is set up to look and feel like a series of pressing decisions, most of which are variations on the theme of pitting communal good against self-interest. And while each of these choices may have immediate, seemingly high-stakes consequences, decisions contestants make have little to no bearing on the show's actual outcome. Short-term drama belies a total absence of strategic possibility. *Bachelor Pad* is like a pinball machine, except its competitors aren't the ones clicking frenetically at the levers — they're just the stock of balls. Under the auspices of taking steps towards victory, they are, in fact, only ever imprisoned in a senseless snarl.

All this to say: if *The Bachelor* is a game show wrapped in a marriage plot, *Bachelor Pad* was a parable of nihilism wrapped in, like, eight different game shows. Its true function (and the dark secret of its appeal) was that it dramatized the ways human beings treat one another when goaded into an erroneous belief in their ability to act with strategic self-interest — when they mistake themselves for free agents turning in a universe graced with some near-tangible order. The show's many layers of contradictory and misdirecting competition were like strips of papier-mâché imbricated over a balloon — a thin, functional cover for what was only ever going to wither limply and recede.

Now just to be clear: if you are a certain kind of *Bachelor* viewer — or just a regular *Bachelor* viewer in a certain kind of mood — *Bachelor Pad* can be a good time. Tenuous and strange and truly vacuous, it delivers a particular kind of fan service, deepening the dimensions of some of the show's most iconic characters, both to their credit and against it.

For instance, without *Bachelor Pad*, Chris Bukowski might have remained an old-fashioned mama-and-papa's boy from good Polish-American Chicago stock who maybe fell a little too hard under Emily Maynard's *Bachelorette* spell. On the *Pad*? Turns out that guy was a party-hardy shitbag waiting to deploy.[67] Sans *Bachelor Pad*, we might have never seen Michael Stagliano blossom from a sweet, attention-deficient man-child into a more flawed but also more interesting grown-ass man. We might never have glimpsed a preview of Michelle Money's

---

67 Though in this case (and in others, but here the feeling is strong), I have to admit that I have some uncomfortable feelings of cause vs. effect. Was the sweet boy who appeared on Emily's season a façade, or did the very experience of being on reality TV itself unleash some dormant, fame-hungry, particularly callous form of sadness?

depthless capacity for straight-shooting narration (to be fully realized on *Paradise*). And we would have been denied the coupling of Kasey and Vienna. She was the villain-winner of Jake's season,[68] and he was the "Guard and Protect Your Heart" guy from Ali's: a one-man boy band, prone to sung-through declarations of affection (not to mention one very ill-advised, very permanent romantic gesture in the form of an actual ink-on-skin tattoo). The Kasey-Vienna meeting of the minds was something special. Watching their hate-mance blossom elicits a feeling that is not quite schadenfreude, but maybe its slightly more affectionately patronizing cousin: that intense squirm of can't look vs. can't look away. Isn't that precisely the feeling reality TV was made for?

Bachelor Pad did not exactly appeal to the romantic faith on which its flagship show is predicated, but it nonetheless delivered something to the *Bachelor*-faithful. And for two seasons, things went more or less as planned: contestants ran around in a tizzy, fucked with one another relentlessly, and believed themselves to be acting in the name of a game. Each time the final couple was faced with their prisoner's dilemma, they mistakenly believed they had arrived at the top by way of shared effort, and both opted to share the prize. For two seasons, *Bachelor Pad* whipped up a concoction of venial backstabbing, betrayal, and blame, but topped things off with a maraschino reminder that sharing is caring.

Not all those cast were fan favorites or villains. The deck

---

68 It's impossible to not mention that Vienna and Jake had what was probably the worst on-air breakup of all time, mediated-slash-goaded by Chris Harrison.

was also cut with wild cards — some of whom producers clearly knew had on-camera potential their first franchise appearances failed to tap, but others who seem to have arrived only by virtue of being made in the right shape and with a hole in their schedule. *Bachelor Pad* took one such flyer on Nick Peterson, best not-remembered for his role as Shirtless Man #4 on Ashley's season of *The Bachelorette*. The gamble on Nick's ability to deliver would prove to be so far wrong, it went all the way right.

For the majority of season three of *Bachelor Pad*, Nick is remaindered: not targeted for elimination, cut out of the action, and, in the minds of those who believe themselves to be at the center of the machine, considered out of the running. But here the arbitrariness of the so-called game slowly comes to light as Nick slips through week after week without cause for remark, only to seemingly materialize among the final pairs when Rachel — who's spent her run in the thick of both romantic and game-related drama — has her love interest and game partner voted off without her and is yoked to Nick by default. Forced together by circumstance, Nick and Rachel head to the final rounds, win no competitions, and, by virtue of this unintimidating showing, bobble through to become the final two left standing. Nick has arrived at the finale having won no challenge, brokered no deal, joined no alliance, and found no love.

At the live-taped finale, Nick and Rachel sit side-by-side on a couch in the center of the stage, each holding a placard concealing their final decision to share the prize or take a shot at stealing it for themselves. Rachel shifts awkwardly and tugs at the hemline of her dress, clutches her placard, leans forward anxiously. Nick sits beside her like a manspreading meme before its time: legs graphically open, weight back, one arm cocked nonchalantly over the back of the seat, edging into Rachel's personal space.

At Chris Harrison's prompting, Rachel rushes quickly through her obligatory recap of her decision-making process, tosses out a platitude about partnership, and reveals her placard with its sans serif, all-caps declarative to SHARE.

Then Nick takes the stage:

Thank you, Rachel, and thank you everybody for the opportunity to be here. I think it's really funny — not necessarily like ha-ha [*high-pitched fake laugh*], knee-slapping funny — but ironic that nobody sitting up there in the cast, nobody sitting here in this audience, and nobody sitting at home watching right now ever would have put their money on me being here to win this. Honestly, they really wouldn't have. I know you wouldn't have. [*he points at Chris Harrison, who fake-chuckles gamely*] It's crazy, though, to sit up here and watch last episode. And to see Jaclyn say that I don't deserve to be here. And to see Ed say I'm just an anonymous guy in the house. It's like, "Ouch, thanks, Ed."

I was on nobody's radar. Nobody was ever on my team. And I did this all myself. Nobody ever cared how I was going to vote. Nobody cared what my plan was. And I feel like I'm an outsider. And I got here by myself and I did this all by myself. Rachel never wanted to be my partner. She didn't. And as a matter of fact, she told me that she backed into this partnership. She tried to leave on me three times. [*he turns to Rachel*] You tried to leave on me three times . . . You knew it was going to screw me over, but it didn't matter. I had to talk to you, and Jaclyn had to talk to you, and you know what you told me? That it was Jaclyn's words that kept you here, not mine.

Here Nick pauses to drum his fingers on the slate that holds his decision. It sounds decidedly plastic and hollow. Rachel tries weakly to insist that she stuck it out with him, but Nick carries on.

NICK: You wanted to do it for Michael. You were on the phone with Michael, you wanted to talk to Michael, you wanted to see Michael. And you know how bad it sucks when you're in the final competition to sing together and you tell me, "If Michael and I were to be in this competition together, we'd win this for sure." But I was your partner.

RACHEL: I didn't say that.

NICK: You sure did. [*he flips the board around, removes the placard quickly*] And so I decided to keep it.

The room explodes. Gasps. Eventually, there is a standing ovation. Nick rushes the small stage in front of him to hug and high-five the dude-bro-iest among the cast. It's an end zone dance. Most of Rachel's response requires bleeping. Chris Harrison declares himself speechless. "You're such a schmuck," Rachel tells Nick through tears.

"I'm a schmuck with $250,000," Nick corrects.

Nick's victory speech is revolutionary and amazing — but also a major hazard. His season-long irrelevance reveals that any random pinball can be flung through the center of the *Bachelor Pad*'s vacuous maze of diversions and obstacles, face none of them, and still sink the jackpot. Not only is Nick's win a reward for not playing by the rules, it's a direct result of being a loser. This threatens to reveal every other character's behavior not only as cruel, but, worse, as senseless: every small and large act of betrayal, unkindness, and deception made along the way is not a by-product of forging a path to greatness, it's a pageant to nothing.

One way the *Bachelor* universe has always justified its own cruelty is by suggesting that heartbreak is a kind of karmic investment. *The Bachelor* and *Bachelorette* insist that those who give themselves over fully to the show's process and wind up sacrificed in the name of someone else's romantic journey may be rewarded in a second onscreen life. Because the show's leads are internal hires, the *Bachelor*'s turnover trains viewers to believe that the first step in a heroic quest is to play the role of tributary to the journey that came before.

So it's worth noting that Rachel's path to sit beside Nick on the *Bachelor Pad* finale couch included being humiliatingly rejected by her game-and-romance partner Michael, who, it comes out, never intended to pursue a real, offscreen relationship. Getting dumped because he's just not that into you isn't quite the same as being willingly devoured by the maw of romantic fate, but, hey, neither is $250,000 the same as a heroic rebirth. Though the terms are different, Bachelor Nation has been trained to assume that, once delivered to the threshold of some kind of recompense, innocent pain will not go unacknowledged. And yet Rachel's does. Not only that, but Nick's recapping of his own marginality is an unmistakable reminder that there are no protagonists here, no heroic journeys to bet on. Rachel is heartbroken and broke, and it's certainly not in the name of love.

Nick's testament to amoral absurdism is one of the best moments the *Bachelor* franchise ever produced. All the drama the show had ever wished for and then some, it was, to a frame, a specimen of perfection. It was also clearly a big fucking problem that needed to be locked down and contained before the mouth-frothing conniption of nihilism could break the skin of the franchise universe and threaten to reach the *Bachelor*'s beating heart. Though it wouldn't be announced for months, *Bachelor Pad* secured its euthanasia the moment Nick collected his first high-five. In a system built on the persistent recycling of heroism, there's zero room for the exaltation of an antihero. And so it was: *Bachelor Pad* must die.

While not exactly a failure, *Bachelor Pad* ultimately proved to veer too far off-brand. For all the ways in which it performed a Spirographic doodling around a fundamental emptiness, its biggest misstep, I would argue, was introducing a name-able sum of cash[69] to what the *The Bachelor* and *Bachelorette* have built up as an economy of sacrifice and reward dealing in affect alone. *Bachelor Pad* contestants were prone to mention the real-life problems $250,000 might solve: children, sick family members, debt. It was a little too real, and a lot too sad. It's worth noting the contrast here with how bummer real-life stories work on *Bachelor* and *Bachelorette*. For all the time those shows spend on trauma, they offer a mollifying narrative about how love is the answer to all problems, a reward for survival. *Bachelor Pad*'s mistake was to draw attention to how fallacious this is by making that reward into an actual cash payout.

Lesson learned: a *Bachelor*-made spectacle is about what happens when you isolate people from real-life conditions. And so the show must draw away from the banal truths of real life, not rely on them for bait. The show's stakes must be — or at least plausibly appear to be — built strictly on human feeling. Differently put: *Bachelor Pad* just wasn't there for the right reasons.

---

69 As opposed to the unacknowledged financial payoff of the show's generation of celebrity, the silence around which is enforced by sentencing anyone who so much as glances towards this truth with a terminal case of "the wrong reasons."

But producers evidently (and rightly) saw something in the *Pad* worth salvaging. After a year's hiatus, the franchise took another stab at an addition to the ABC summer lineup that would service fans with further tales of their favorite *Bachelor* alumni. In 2013, we were graced with *Bachelor in Paradise*.

It's a literal departure: rather than further corrupt any associations with the iconic L.A. County mansion, *Bachelor in Paradise* sweeps us away to the promised land of a Mexican beach resort, complete with off-season flourishes of comically hazardous meteorology and low-key infestations of fauna.[70] There, the show strips down, dispensing with *Bachelor Pad*'s Rube Goldberg–like fuss — no contests, no immunity, no money. *Paradise* is pure: just a gaggle of *Bachelor* and *Bachelorette* contestants hooking up, looking for love, and getting in one another's way. Though stretched into many more weeks' worth of broadcastable material, the whole thing is filmed in around three weeks.

Here's how it works: each episode, rose-ceremonial power lies with either the men or the women, who give their token long-stem or boutonnière to a member of the opposite sex with whom they see romantic potential. When the men are handing out roses, there is a surplus of women, and the next week, vice versa. The numbers are kept competitive with the cycling in of new contestants bearing date cards and the opportunity to ask someone out (thus testing any prior, rose-ceremony-made bonds that person might have formed).

---

70 So many crabs.

As the show nears its end, any couples left standing are sent on fantasy suite overnight dates and issued a stern warning from Chris Harrison to move on to the final rose ceremony only if their love is deeply felt enough to bring the relationship out of *Paradise* and back down to Earth. On the first season, when we've never before seen where this is going, Harrison's exhortation is so forbidding that it seems like the dubious reward for hanging on until the end may be that couples will be forced into legal matrimony on the spot. This does not prove to be the case, though each season has managed to produce at least one marriage proposal.[71]

The *Pad*-to-*Paradise* transition should be written up in business school curricula as a case study in precision branding through product upgrades.[72] For all the notes *Bachelor Pad* squawked in the wrong key, early *Paradise*[73] would spin a melody pitched to resonate almost unnervingly at some marrow-deep, *Bachelor*-bred tuning. Call it the opposite of the "don't know what you've got till it's gone" effect: sometimes you don't know what you need till it's there.

---

71 Six proposals in four seasons have yielded: two broken engagements; one ongoing engagement; two aired weddings; and one fake on-air wedding that was never ratified and, now that the couple has broken up, never spoken of again. Not to mention the first babes born of Generation Paradise: Jade and Tanner Tolbert had a girl in 2017, and Carly and Evan Bass are expecting a girl in early 2018.

72 Did you go to business school? If so, you might have already guessed from this sentence that I did not. If "precision branding" isn't a thing, it totally should be.

73 By which I mean the first three seasons of the show. We'll get to season four later in the chapter.

The main lesson *Paradise* learned from its predecessor: poke fun. Where *Pad* was real trash, *Paradise* is pure camp. Its mirth is democratic, and with everything and everyone up for being mocked, there is an equal opportunity for those who make, watch, and perform the show to be in on the joke. Where *Pad* managed to be at once vacuous and self-serious, *Paradise* is the inverse, making good on the drama, but always quick to turn to the side and give a cartoonish wink and a smile.[74] *Bachelor Pad* concealed the dark absurdity of nihilism — *Paradise* splashes absurdity front and center in a saturated, tropical palette.

Ironically, this overall tonal shift towards frivolity makes room for the show to work its way into deeper, more convincing moments of seriousness when it chooses to do so. It's just like the increased visibility of production on *The Bachelor* and *Bachelorette*, only here taken to aesthetic extremes. The franchise has got it figured out: emotional sincerity is more recognizable when produced in a context that celebrates the artificial rather than denying it.

Bachelor in Paradise is truly an example of unscripted genius, and if I was able to scrounge up a few winning gestures from *Bachelor Pad* in a paragraph, it would take a whole chapter to enumerate all the gifts brought forth from the first seasons of *Paradise*. This is true of form as well as content: the show may get contestants in a pretty disinhibited state of sun-soaked

74 I mean that quite literally: in the show's opening credit sequence, contestants' winks and smiles are sometimes animated with twinkles and underscored with comic pings.

partying, but it's just as much "Producers Gone Wild." Take, for example, the *Paradise* innovation I'll dub the creature confessional: a scene in which a contestant is edited so as to appear to be in intimate dialogue with Mexican-beach-dwelling wildlife. Now that it's become a staple, it's easy to forget, I think, just how truly damning and hilarious it was the first time we watched high-maintenance contestant Clare Crawley appear to yell-cry "This is fucking drama!" to a raccoon. By season three, just as the animal trope seems like it may have run its course, the bit digs yet self-referentially deeper when Ashley I., who has been made to seem as though she is sobbing her romantic frustrations to a parrot, laugh-cries to her interlocutor: "You know they're going to make you into a raccoon."

Paradise was also the source of the only dramatic re-enactment the show has ever seen fit to produce. In season one, contestant Michelle K., she of the cast-for-being-batshit variety, sent herself home under mysterious circumstances on the very first night. The next week, the show had the pleasure of revealing that Michelle had hooked up with a member of the crew (a sound guy improbably named Ryan Putz) in pre-filming downtime. When producers came knocking at Michelle's door while Putz was in the room, the sound man jumped from her balcony so as not to be found fraternizing with the talent. The drop to the ground was 25 feet, and Putz broke both his legs. On this one, *Paradise* delivers, telling the tale through soft-edged dramatic re-enactment, interviews with witnesses, and narration by Chris Harrison (who may be fully torqued while telling this ridiculous story).

Alas, it would be downright oppressive to recap all of *Paradise*'s gems for you. Had I time and space, I would wax rhapsodic about Michelle Money's genius for clear, stylish communication. I'd sing of Daniel the Canadian's predilection for metaphorical vehicles plucked from 20th-century history, outer space, and ornithology. I would hold up the two minutes in which one of the indistinguishable Vegas twins winds up impossibly wasted off exactly half a bottle of beer as the most endearing day-drunkenness ever captured on film. And speaking of two-for-one sister deals, I would recommend taking in the time Ashley I. brought her younger sister to *Paradise* as a security blanket so the sisters could exhibit their unique brand of propping one another up with ruthless negging. Iaconetti the Younger may have spoilsported her way through *Paradise*, but her gift to us was the image left as she exited the show petulantly dragging a rolling suitcase through wet sand. What a hero.

Paradise can also warp perception of characters we thought we knew and loved. Take, for instance, Joe from Kaitlyn's season: on the *Bachelorette* he was the dry, crass class clown from Kentucky with an oddly sexy Neanderthal thing going for him. Under influence of *Paradise*, we see Joe as one half of *The Bachelor*'s answer to the Macbeths. We discover that Joe is so skilled a manipulator that when Jonathan tries to call him out on a lie, things get so turned around that the grown man winds up begging Joe's forgiveness and weeping in deeply felt shame. "I made him my bitch," Joe concludes. (Be sure to put a deep Kentucky twang on that when you play it in your head.)

And then there are those who arrive as villains to descend but further still — some to comedic effect, and others less so. Chris Bukowski delivers a few good moments in his 30-some-odd hours in Paradise: just long enough to tear the meniscus in his knee, get peaceably boggled on pain killers, and go home with a woman with an upsetting capacity for delusion and suggestibility. Would not surprise me if he woke up the next day without a clue who she was.

Another villain who failed to rehab during a *Paradise* stint measured in hours rather than days is Chad from JoJo's season. Chad put on a real bed-shitting[75] by getting blackout drunk, fall-down violent, and inclined to mumble-sling offensive slurs.[76] The gossamer-thin strand of silver to tease out of what is otherwise an exclusively depressive performance: Chad's behavior leads to one of the only times I can remember that the show has ever actually addressed misogyny, when Sarah Herron (total mensch, member of that most rarified strata of *Bachelor* good peeps) tells Chad off for his abuse. It's a stand up and cheer kind of moment, but I don't know if I'd argue that it's worth the price of admission.[77]

Last but not least, if I were really, properly giving the show its due, I would try to convince you that for a very few

---

75 This is possibly literal: cast members allege that after he passes out on a heap of sand for the night, Chad craps his pants in his sleep.

76 It's a level of obliterated that feels extremely uncomfortable to watch — the kind of thing where it's suddenly just a little too obvious that alcohol is actual poison.

77 Again, also not worth the ticket price, but I do have to note that as he's kicked off the show, Chad's ire delivers a gift to us as he randomly turns on Chris Harrison and berates the host with the accusation "You went to sleep last night with a mimosa and a robe on!" If not an end that justifies the means, it's an image I'll never quite shake.

couples locked down in the *Paradise* pressure cooker, their love is amazingly, improbably, the real deal.[78] Color me a believer.

Paradise will always be secondary to the original shows, if for nothing else than its dependence on them to provide its cast of pre-made characters. More and more, however, influence travels in both directions, and *Paradise* has begun to exert its celestial influence on the main stage.

Now, along with casting women and men who show potential as love interests, controversy bait, or villains, *The Bachelor* and *Bachelorette* proper turn up examples of a certain kind of amenable screwball who, in the past, would almost certainly have been deemed too offbeat or lightweight to be taken far on the *Bachelor* journey. This special class of citizen is earmarked for *Paradise*, transcending right and wrong reasons altogether: benevolent but impermanent, a figure merely way-stationing on a producer-blessed ascent to their true celestial home.[79] While I don't think *Paradise* will ever generate the gravitational pull necessary to upend the established order and turn the *Bachelor* universe into a binary system,[80] with each of its first three seasons, *Paradise* shed just a little bit more of its sideshow identity.

---

78 Notably Tanner and Jade, of course, but also Carly and Evan, who really do seem to have frickin' found their frickin' way to a love match made for true dorks. Plus Taylor and Derek, who may prove to have less franchise staying power than the other two couples, but do seem in it to win it as far as their partnership goes.

79 Examples include Ashley S. on Chris's season, Daniel the Canadian on JoJo's, and Alexis a.k.a. "The Dolphin" on Nick's.

80 A third show, *The Bachelor Winter Games*, coinciding with the 2018 Winter Olympics, promises to feature contestants pulled from some of the 22 international versions of *The Bachelor* along with *Pad*-style competitions.

For all that, there is only one story to be told of *Paradise* lost and won — or won through loss may be more like it. Because if *Bachelor Pad*'s defining set piece was in its elevation of Nick Whatshisname[81] to the heights of antiheroism, the power of *Bachelor in Paradise* is revealed in the propulsion of a different Nick around a different iteration of fortune's wheel.

We've talked about Nick Viall in previous chapters, but to put the pieces together in one place, a recap: Nick arrived on Andi Dorfman's season of *The Bachelorette* in 2012 as a boyish, mumbly Midwestern software salesman. A 34-year-old in plaid and Converse, he was possessed of a carriage — a particular kind of downcast toe-scuffing that's equal parts appearance and attitude — that benefited hugely from the mid-aughts exaltation of hipster man-childishness. A self-proclaimed skeptic of the *Bachelor* process, and prone, as Andi puts it, to get "salty" on group dates, Nick was cast as the season's villain on the strength of his inability to get along with the other guys.

But Andi liked him a lot. Nick went to fantasy suites, and then to final two. Before he could pick out a ring to propose with,[82] Andi cut him off at the pass and dumped him. And he might have stayed there — a villain walked back just a bit by

---

81 Yes, his last name is Peterson, but Whatshisname just suits him, you know? Nick P. actually returns in *Paradise* to "find love" with Samantha, who was almost completely edited out of Chris Soules's *Bachelor* season only to turn up in *Paradise* as a villain with big-time dead-inside vibes. She and Nick apparently had in common a prehensile urge to continue consuming resources and occupying space. No one cared about their love even a little.

82 For all the complaints from the other men about Nick's sincerity, once he overcame the hurdle of his initial skepticism, Nick's intention to marry the Bachelorette did not seem in any way feigned to me.

the sympathy of late-stage rejection — but instead Nick used his time with Andi on "After the Final Rose" to highlight the fact that in the fantasy suite, the lead sometimes sleeps with the loser too. And thus Nick secured himself in the hearts and minds of Bachelor Nation with the shame of being both a villain and a sook.[83]

A year later, when the *The Bachelorette* had moved on with Kaitlyn Bristowe, Nick turned up midway through the season, appearing alongside a few other franchise alumni in the live audience on one of Kaitlyn's group dates. Unlike the members of the *Bachelor* fam he came with, he wasn't just there to watch the suitors rap battle: having gotten cozy in Kaitlyn's DMs before filming, Nick wanted to catch the now-Bachelorette IRL and see if there might be something there. Kaitlyn bent the rules to admit him to her dating pool, and Nick wound up lapping the pack. Here the advantage of being an experienced contestant really showed: Nick's fluency in *Bachelor*-think and filming conditions made him come off downright comfy in moments when the other contestants flailed. It was as though we were watching an age-progressed version of the boy-child who'd wooed Andi Dorfman the year before.

Still, across Bachelor Nation, reviews of Nick remained mixed. This is in part, of course, the result of some off-schedule, non-fantasy-suite sex you might remember from Chapter 2. For viewers who objected to that change of itinerary, being party to this transgression made Nick at the very least an accessory

---

83 I've never understood why people thought this was such an underhanded thing to do to Andi — to me it's always just seemed like a very embarrassing thing for Nick to do to himself.

to *Bachelor* sin. He took some heat. Say, like, four degrees off Kaitlyn's pyre.[84]

Whether charmer or charlatan, Nick Viall's second time through the *Bachelorette* gamut yielded results similar to the first: final two, thinks he's the one, turns out he isn't. This time, he gets one excruciating step further: he's most of the way through a proposal speech and just about to whip out a Neil Lane retina-burner to seal the deal when Kaitlyn finally stops him. "No? Alright," he says quietly with his face not yet detached from the nervous proposal grin, lagging a beat behind his evident awareness. It's pretty rough.[85]

On his first crack at the franchise can, Nick caught the eye of one of the brainiest Bachelorettes to date, and on round two, he connected with the funniest and coolest. With each *Bachelor* spin, Nick was accruing endorsements, making himself worth a closer look. By the time he is driven away from his failed proposal to Kaitlyn and appraises himself as "the world's biggest joke," it seems inevitable that he should go forth to frolic in the happy hunting ground for punchlines.

Washing up on the beaches of *Paradise* in 2016, it's Nick's third *Bachelor* appearance in as many years. We've known

---

84 It wasn't just the mouthy misogynists who didn't appreciate Viall 2.0. Devoted members of Team Shawn B. (now Kaitlyn's fiancé and from all appearances true love) may have wondered whether the more-than-usually-elevated animosity between the rivals held some special significance. Something in the way the future Mr. Kaitlyn Bristowe seemed to truly next-level *hate* Nick's very being hinted at something perhaps elided from the viewer's vantage — some fact or feature of Nick's time on the show left out of view.

85 Kaitlyn, for her part, seems to be suffering badly enough in this scene to very nearly justify medical attention. From the way she keeps her face clenched in a frozen grimace from the moment Nick starts speaking, I have to think that suffering this proposal is a term of some agreement struck between the Bachelorette and production. If I was being cynical, I might suggest that it's a line item of her sex-penance.

him as the villain and as "the other guy,"[86] seen him wheedle around rules, sulk in corners, undercut alpha crowds with beta savvy. Twice we've watched him get his heart broken, and twice we've heard evidence — of both the reported and recorded variety — of his getting it on. In *Paradise*, he is identified onscreen with the simple tag line "Runner-Up."

It may not have been a straightforward upward trajectory, but with each *Bachelor* appearance, Nick was pulling into crisper focus. He was also literally becoming more sharply cut: clothes, hair, abs, jib. Nick looks like he's weathered a few *Bachelor* offseasons hibernating in a CrossFit cave, emerging as a man just shy of his 36th birthday with, like, seven-and-half percent body fat, tops. A would-be Gen-Xer finding himself as a late-blooming Millennial, Nick has devoted his middle thirties to getting really good at selfies and getting dumped on TV.

Still, for all that, I don't think anyone could have predicted just how squarely in Nick's wheelhouse *Paradise* would prove to be. I don't so much mean that it's his best light for romance (that distinction goes to Jared Haibon[87]) — more that Nick would reveal himself to be more holistically attuned to *Paradise*'s patterns than other contestants, better equipped to catch its drift.

Here's the thing: reality TV rewards a very particular kind of intelligence. It's not uncommon to see *Bachelor* and

---

86 A Shawn Booth coinage designed, presumably, to deny his nemesis power.

87 Jared set the trend of a phenomenon wherein someone who appears to be of average attractiveness in the context of their *Bachelor/ette* season becomes a top-shelf commodity in *Paradise*.

Bachelorette contestants with qualities born of higher order intuition: social acuity, kindness, canniness, cunning. The kinds of smart that allow a person to vibe what's happening around them and lock into its pocket. But a certain kind of deconstructive, arm's-length braininess that favors the critical tends not to make it on the show in the first place, and when it does, it's usually a pretty big impediment. *The Bachelor* demands wholesale participation, a two-heeled jump motored by faith, not reason. To think is to unravel. Those who indulge the urge often ruminate themselves right off the show.[88] Nick Viall isn't a MacArthur-level outlier or anything, but he does appear to be a healthy standard deviation or two away from the *Bachelor* mean. I'd say he's rocking about the peak level of analytic intelligence a contestant can possess before it's an unavoidable disqualifier.[89]

If I was going to diagnose the source of viewers' distaste for Nick Viall, I'd say it comes from his squirmy, effortful calculation. Even at his most stripped down and exposed — even when his brokenness and shame are apparently genuine — Nick often maintains a whiff of something disingenuous that, under the conditions of *The Bachelorette*, he just couldn't seem to shake no matter how chill he behaved. It took going

---

88 Think, for example, of Sharleen Joynt, that pillar of Canadian class who appeared on Juan Pablo's season. "I wish I was a little dumber," Sharleen admits to Juan Pablo, "so I could just be like: duhhh. That would be so much nicer." Sharleen ultimately sent herself home after conceding that a "cerebral connection" with the Bachelor just wasn't there.

89 In fact, had he been chasing just about any other Bachelorette in the first place, Nick would probably have neurotically waffled himself off the show as well. But Andi was right there with him, always quick to praise their "mental connection" as part and parcel of the attraction. In the end, when she breaks up with him, Andi cites their mutually catalyzing critical minds, the exhaustion of "overanalyzing every single moment."

to a place where the superficial is the rule for Nick to thrive. In *Paradise*, that irksome self-consciousness suddenly seemed more like self-awareness. And if Nick was the world's biggest joke, he could easily break down his own structure for you, but he'd also be quick to cue an empty laugh track to please the audience. That is to say, like *Paradise* itself, Nick is more or less exactly equally smart *and* superficial.

The three weeks in *Paradise* were Nick Viall's rehabilitation program, revealing his ability to tap the show's full emotional range, navigating deftly between complete self-mocking and genuine feeling. Take, for example, Nick talking to his main *Paradise* squeeze as she presses him on the fact that he is holding back emotional commitment: "I am self-conscious of the fact that I'm the guy who basically would have been engaged to two different girls. If I jump in again, then I become, like, a Trivial Pursuit question." It's a hilarious and damning allusion, but rather than play it for yuks, this is a moment in which Nick is being shown as truly vulnerable. We see that he gets the joke, *and* we feel for him as a result. Nick is uniquely attuned to *Paradise*'s gifts and thus able to fully reap its benefits, sometimes, as this example shows, even in the same moment.

There are also instances in *Paradise* in which Nick's ability to both view a situation from the outside and be in it make him an ideal candidate for being the audience's proxy. In his interactions with lugubrious Ashley I., for example, Nick is both a tough-loving real pal and a calm voice of viewers' frustrations. On Ashley's mulish pursuing of Jared, Nick gives her the goods:

NICK: This isn't love. It's infatuation and obsession.

ASHLEY: It's love!

NICK: No, it's not. Not even close. You will never be with Jared.

ASHLEY: [*sobbing*] You can't tell me that!

Some episodes later, when Ashley professes to have turned her frown upside down, Nick is again in fine form, giving her exactly the words of encouragement she's earned: "I . . . believe in you?"

There are many paths to becoming a villain, but really there is only one way out: to ascend to the rank of hero. As *Paradise* went on and Nick become more and more of a fan favorite, the show took a chance and made a last-minute call, swapping out the Bachelor they'd cast and bringing in an unlikely ringer. Nick — one-time villain, two-time sexcapader, all-time runner-up record holder — was rotated out of the mire of his past and carried into the future on the wings of *Paradise*.

When I set out to explore how the first three seasons of *Bachelor in Paradise* expanded the franchise's aesthetic reach by fixing its tongue firmly in cheek, the last thing last thing I expected was that in season four, *Paradise* would get way too real.

In June 2017, reports emerged that *Paradise* had suspending filming due to allegations of sexual misconduct on set. A third-party complaint was filed by a producer who questioned whether Corinne Olympios was capable of consenting to a sexual encounter with fellow cast member DeMario Jackson. The event in question was, of course, captured by the show's ever-present cameras.

A full-blown scandal bloomed: named and unnamed sources came forward with conflicting reports of who and what and when and with what knowledge. Both Corinne and DeMario lawyered up and issued statements. Her: "I am a victim . . . As a woman, this is my worst nightmare and it has now become my reality." Him: "It's unfortunate that my character and family name has been assassinated this past week with false claims and malicious allegations."

Ten days after shutting down production, Warner Bros. announced that it had conducted an internal investigation in consultation with an outside law firm and found no evidence of wrongdoing. *Paradise* would go ahead with a curtailed filming schedule and slightly later release date.

Corinne's team later concluded their own investigation with a statement in which Corinne clarified her previous position, saying she "felt victimized by the fact that others were judging me through conflicting and unsubstantiated reports, while I myself had no recollection of the events that transpired . . . My team's investigation into this matter has now been completed to my satisfaction." She was invited to return to *Paradise* but respectfully declined.

My interest is not in adjudicating what occurred on the set of *Bachelor in Paradise*, but in considering how the show depicted these events onscreen. And in order to do that, we have to harken back a bit. Because the incident — messy enough on its face — was further complicated by the roles Corinne and DeMario played in their previous *Bachelor* and *Bachelorette* appearances.

DeMario had been eliminated from the most recent season of *The Bachelorette* in a cloud of old-school villainy when producers delivered a woman to set claiming that DeMario was her recent (or maybe current) boyfriend.[90] After a *Springer*-style confrontation, DeMario was sent home a disgrace and a liar.[91]

In her appearance on Nick Viall's *Bachelor* season, Corinne was pegged as a villain because she couldn't lie *enough* to fall in line and play nice with others. Unafraid to take what she wanted or demand someone provide her with it,[92] Corinne's villainy (such as it was) took the form of sloppy, petulant hedonism. She was a creature of many comforts: scarfing hors d'oeuvres at cocktail parties, sloshing fat glasses of wine (always sparkling) during interviews, and luxuriating in bubble baths. One of her most memorable crimes against the show's mores occurred when she skipped a rose ceremony because

---

90 I don't recommend bothering with this episode if you haven't already been subjected to it; however, I *do* recommend the gif of DeMario's reaction shot upon seeing his alleged gf. His attempt to transition from obvious recognition to "Who's this?" is priceless.

91 Rachel's cue to DeMario to exit: "I'm not here to be played, I'm not here to be made a joke of . . . so I'm really going to need you to get the fuck out."

92 Recall from Chapter 3 that 24-year-old Corinne is proud to have a nanny.

she'd crawled off somewhere to take what looked to me like a sticky, champagne-sodden nap.

As a villain of excess, Corinne's appetites were also, naturally, sexual. She regularly conjured scenarios of varying degrees of explicitness to play out with Nick, regardless of whether the other women were present (exhorting Nick to fondle her naked breasts during a group date photo shoot, straddling him in a bouncy castle, encouraging him to lick whipped cream off her chest). On one occasion, she pulled a Courtney Robertson original and turned up at the Bachelor's door to seduce him during off-hours. (Having learned from his time with Kaitlyn Bristowe, Nick stuck to the *Bachelor* rules of engagement and sent her back to her own room about as kindly as is possible when turning someone down for sex.)

My point here is that *Bachelor in Paradise* didn't just have a sex scandal to account for, but an imbroglio made especially murky by the involvement of characters the show had previously established and benefitted from: the golden promiscuous lush, the charming lying scoundrel. Which is not to suggest that Corinne and DeMario had no agency in cultivating these *Bachelor* personae,[93] but rather that the roles forged symbiotically between these cast members and the franchise were now, for all involved, huge liabilities.

Once it had been given the all-clear (by itself), the show was free to go ahead and do what it does: cue the dramatic soundtrack. And so it goes that *Bachelor in Paradise* season

---

93 Corinne in particular was very much an agent: she grew more delightful as the season went on and emerged from her time on the show as a full-on brand.

four opens on a montage of the familiar *Paradise* sites looking hauntingly abandoned. We linger on a tableau of sun chaises in want of beach bods to cradle, a ladder and tarp abandoned across a path, a pile of packed-up lounge cushions, while the echoing, ghostly voices of newscasters fade and in and out, resonating over words like "allegations," "investigation," and, of course, "trouble in Paradise."

Chris Harrison arrives and gives us his spiel, promising that we will see "everything" that happened in the first two days of filming before production was cut short. And so with a "two weeks earlier" title card, the show rewinds to air its pre-scandal footage, charting the initial *Paradise* arrival. This includes Corinne showing up with two hefty flutes of champagne, offering Chris Harrison cheers as she makes her way down to the beach. It includes the women talking about how DeMario is a liar and a douchebag. We see Corinne and DeMario meet at the bar, take shots, and flirt. She jumps into his arms. "We're on the same page here," she tells him. Later, toasted and giddy, the two of them jump into a pool with their clothes on while another cast member standing nearby narrates their actions.

The next night, heading into what would have been the first rose ceremony, Corinne and DeMario are, to their apparent surprise, whisked away by producers. The rest of the cast looks on in bewilderment as a crew member makes the sign to cut. The cameras point to the ground and film the sand, and the episode trails off in confusion and chaos, leaving the fate of *Paradise* dangling off the edge of a cliff.

What's shocking about all of this is not that it's different, but that it's totally typical. The *Bachelor* dramatic content delivery system only has one dial, and it's always cranked to 11. The machine is not capable of distinguishing between an Archie caught between Betty and Veronica and an allegation of on-set sexual assault. They're both just reasons to stay tuned, stick around, find out why Chris Harrison really *means* it this time when he says this "will go down in *Bachelor* history as the most shocking and, yes, the most dramatic season ever."

In episode two, we pick up once again with Chris Harrison alone on the beach, promising that *Paradise* will soon be revisited. But before we can get to that, first it's time for the marriage of Carly Waddell and Evan Bass, last season's love match. Complete with a supercut of vows exchanged on previous franchise weddings, it's a 45-minute-long advertisement for *The Bachelor*'s softer side. A reminder of what this show is *really* all about: its ability to engineer fairy tale fates.

Presumably the hope is that a saccharine taste will linger in viewers' mouths long enough to get us through what comes next: the cast (minus DeMario and Corinne) trudges down the beach and assembles before Chris Harrison for some real talk. And here, under the auspices of total, frank disclosure, the show does a dizzying series of pirouettes. After reiterating several times and from several perspectives that *nothing bad happened* and letting the cast gush about how real everyone is and how much they love the producers and how much they hate the media meanies, Harrison asks the group: "Do you think race played a part in this?" After a long silence and some stuttering starts and stops, they chime in to confirm that yes, unfortunately it did.

Of course it *does* matter that DeMario is Black and Corinne is white — and the particularly insidious form of racism haunting how the situation was read *should* be unpacked. But for 15 years, *The Bachelor* hasn't given two shits how Black men are portrayed or discriminated against, and if they're willing to get up in arms about it now, that's a testament to the show's depthless, thirsty canniness. The show is angling us into position to force a choice between hashtag causes: you can either believe women, or you can know Black lives matter. Take your pick.

In her official statement on the matter, Corinne reminded us that she had never launched any accusation of her own (remember: the complaint was made by a third party, who never makes an appearance in any of these disclosures). And, when Corinne is given the chance to tell her story in a sit-down with Chris Harrison later in the season,[94] she explains that when she arrived on the set of *Paradise*, she was taking prescription medication that she did not realize doesn't mix with alcohol. The result was a blackout state that *looked* just like a lucid good time. "Everybody thought I was just having fun and being Corinne. There's no way that you guys could have known I was mentally checked out. I don't think it's anyone's fault, but it was an annoying, unfortunate situation," she says.

And thus we have this strange quandary: a crime with many victims, but no perpetrators. Corrine does not blame

---

94 DeMario has his own interview with Harrison in another episode.

DeMario, and DeMario does not blame Corinne, and no one blames the show. The third-party complainant is left as a mysterious lacuna. And so as it performs a defanging on itself, *Paradise* points to one set of snapping jaws everyone involved has agreed did no good: the media.

It was reported that after the shutdown, *Bachelor in Paradise* implemented new policies regarding alcohol consumption and the dispensation of prescription drugs, and requiring a go-ahead from producers before heading into the sex cabana. But none of that was outlined in what was aired. Instead, after giving them a pop quiz on consent,[95] Harrison locks eyes with each member of the cast one by one to ask whether they would like to continue with the show. Thumbs up across the board. "With the power vested in me, I now declare *Bachelor in Paradise* back open," Harrison announces.

Everyone cheers. And then they head to the bar.

My favorite part of *Bachelor in Paradise*'s fourth season happened every episode, every week — a vignette which, in a few short frames, managed to capture the show's robustly ironic, confusing, telling self-image.

In the first verse of the show's burrowing earworm of a theme song, we see Chris Harrison run down the beach in a trim, well-made suit, clutching a bright orange rescue can in one hand and splashing urgently through the frothy churn of

---

95 Chris Harrison: Can someone give consent when they're passed out? Group: No! Chris Harrison: Can someone give consent when they're drunk? Group: [*silence*].

ocean on sand. He cuts across the screen, on a mission too pressing to look at the camera.

At the end of the song, on the final crooning notes of the last call to "Paaaaaradiiiiise," we return to find Harrison again. Still dry, still ashore, he worriedly scans the ocean through binoculars, lifeguard equipment dangling unused from the other hand. The rescue never happened. No one has been saved.

Then he spots us. A switch flips, and Chris Harrison is our host again — he smiles for the camera, opening his arms in easy, carefree welcome. No emergency, no worries, no threat. We're in *Paradise*.

7

Not Going to Say the Words: Race

A beautiful woman gets out of a carriage, nestles a violin into the crook of her neck, and draws a classical riff across the strings of her instrument, making eyes at a handsome man as she glides towards him over cobblestones.

"Hello there," she says as she approaches, putting down her bow. "I'm Shamiqua."

Someone yells and the cameras cut. A bell rings. The fantasy grinds to a halt.

These are the opening seconds of *UnREAL*, the scripted series about producing a *Bachelor*-like reality show. Having stopped the action, Quinn, the lead producer of *UnREAL*'s show-within-a-show, berates an underling for staging this entrance: "Shamiqua? That's your girl? That's the one you said had wife potential? She's *Black* . . . First girl out of the carriage is always a wifey, and that is not wifey."

"There's a Black man in the White House," producer Jay (himself a Black man) reminds her.

"He's barely Black," Quinn says. "It is not my fault America's racist, people . . . Get a new girl out here."

And thus, 90 seconds in, *UnREAL* had done something *The Bachelor* couldn't in over a decade: admitted that Black contestants don't stand a chance.

The first season of *UnREAL* aired in 2014. The next year, the show doubled down on the provocation and built a season arc around casting *Everlasting*'s first Black lead. (On *Everlasting*, this role is called the Suitor.) *UnREAL*'s protagonist, Rachel, is literally orgasmic with self-congratulation at having achieved this milestone. "We're going to make history!" she tells herself breathlessly while fucking a member of the soon-to-be Suitor's entourage at a boozy, blow-filled Vegas celebration to seal the deal.

Later, Rachel and Quinn try to sell the network president on their choice:

NETWORK PRESIDENT: He's Black!

RACHEL: Yeah, he's the first Black Bach—

QUINN: [*interrupting*] No, he's not *that* Black . . . He's like football Black.

The line is cut short, but make no mistake: Rachel was about to say "Bachelor."

In 2012, two Black men from Nashville — Nathaniel Claybrooks and Christopher Johnson — sued ABC for discrimination on *The Bachelor*. As court documents point out, both men had *Bachelor*-ready résumés, and yet, they allege, they were overlooked during the casting process in favor of white applicants.

One of the things that makes the discrimination suit interesting is that it forces to the surface a basic question about what the show *is*. The plaintiffs' case doesn't treat the show as a search for love, but rather as a prolonged job application for next season's lead. The complaint charges that people of color are systematically "denied the same opportunity as their white counterparts to compete for the role of the Bachelor and Bachelorette due to their race and/or color." The whole argument is framed as being about the right to contract. In the end, ABC won the decision (first amendment, etc.). The class action may consider *The Bachelor* an employment opportunity, but the decision against them treats it as an artistic product.

Nobody was fucking around with this suit: the plaintiffs' attorney, George E. Barrett (now deceased), was a prominent civil rights lawyer known for a decades-long battle over integrating higher education in Tennessee. Barrett described his role in the law as a form of social engineering. Evidently, he thought *The Bachelor*'s problem with racial representation was real, and he thought it mattered. In the complaint submitted to the state, Barrett charges the show with the responsibility to answer to something more than the letter of the law regarding the plaintiffs' rights. "[The] defendants have the opportunity to help normalize minority and interracial relationships by showcasing them to mainstream America," he writes. "Instead, by discriminatorily refusing to cast people of color . . . [the defendants] play into the perceived racial fears of their audience and perpetuate outdated racial taboos."

The Bachelor's problem with racial representation is longstanding and well documented. A quick trip down Google lane turns up articles and blog posts and think pieces devoted to tallying minority contestants and detailing their fates on the show. One informal number crunch determined that up to 2016, there had been a total of 36 Black contestants on the show (out of around 775 total contestants), more than half (59%) of whom went home within two weeks. Furthermore, for an unbroken string of seven seasons between 2009 and 2011, not one Black contestant appeared on either *The Bachelor* or *The Bachelorette*. That's zero out of 185 people.

I won't be fact-checking any of those counts, though, nor will I be contributing my own. I find these statistics useful as a means of exposing just how intractable *The Bachelor*'s whitewashed casting habits are, but I'm reluctant to scroll through *Bachelor* and *Bachelorette* class photos scanning faces for evidence of racial coding. Plus, of course, it's not like diverse casting is just a question of Black and white. When the show's issues with racial diversity are raised, someone will inevitably point out, for example, that Bachelor Juan Pablo Galavis is from Venezuela, that Catherine Giudici (winner of Sean Lowe's season) is Filipina-American, or that Bachelorette JoJo Fletcher's mother is Iranian.

This is not to say that *The Bachelor* has ever showed any degree of remote empathy, understanding, or nuance when it comes to its treatment of any marginalized racial or ethnic group. It certainly hasn't. But *The Bachelor* is a show that reflects, above all, America and the American psyche, and the world in which it does so is one that thrives on binary oppositions. So while other kinds of diversity, be it racial or cultural, are treated with a relatively benign, empty-headed obliviousness, the Black-white racial binary that dominates American racial identity manifests more frequently and ominously on *The Bachelor*.

As I've discussed in previous chapters, one way *The Bachelor* maintains sovereignty is through its language — a dialect that translates emotions, issues, and social conditions into easily digestible phrases and symbols. This way of speaking is a necessary adaptation — a strategy for reaching through the punishing and unreal state of making reality TV to achieve something like intimacy. On set, *Bachelor*-talk is indeed the language of love.

But here's the thing: there is no word for "Black" in *Bachelor*ese. As a result, contestants who try to talk about racial issues either risk that the blunt force of their vocabulary will tamper with the show's hermetic seal, or else find themselves in a frustrated tizzy of obliquity, gesture, and approximation.

Take, for example, contestant Kupah James on Kaitlyn's season of *The Bachelorette*. This is 2015, so it's a few seasons out from the notorious three-year moratorium on casting Black people, but contestants who look like Kupah still remain few. Here's the sitch: Kupah's made it past night one and has participated in one group date (where Kaitlyn felt he made no effort to show interest in her). Going into the rose ceremony, Kupah talks to another contestant, Jonathan, about where he stands (they make up two of the three Black contestants still in the competition):

KUPAH: [*gestures to his face*] I don't know if she sees me as much as she sees other guys. Clearly, three roses [handed out already] — I'm not one of them. Same with you, right?

JONATHAN: Yeah, I'm not one of them right now.

KUPAH: I don't know what she [*passing hand over his face*] *sees* in me.

In an ITM with producers, Kupah is more explicit: "I don't want to be here any longer than I have to be if — *if*, if — I'm the minority guy that fills a quota."

At this point in the competition, Kupah has, like many contestants in the still-deep dating pool, barely spoken to the

Bachelorette. Unlike others who share this position, however, he has to be suspicious about that lack of contact. White contestants have the privilege of assuming that if they're still around in spite of a lack of time with Kaitlyn, that's a testament to innate good qualities she only has yet to uncover. Kupah has to worry that it's about production's desire to save face by exploiting his.

With these clips lined up nicely for us, viewers know what's on Kupah's mind. When he tries to address his concerns with Kaitlyn, however, he starts out low-key accusing her of not paying enough attention to him, and then eventually gets to this:

> I guess it's just important to me that you do see me in the group of men that are here . . . Because there are some things about me that matter a lot — one of them would be not only substance and personality, but also there are some things that are unfortunate, but things I have to think about as a person. And that's, like, I don't want to be here because I look good on the roster of men that you're still — that you still keep around.

Based on her reaction, I'd wager that Kaitlyn has no idea what Kupah is driving at. To be fair to her, they're a few drinks deep, and he's getting into word-salad territory. To be fair to *him*, if his language is oblique, well, he's wading into *Bachelor* taboo. Rather than being able to assert the moral righteousness of his own intentions, Kupah has to flip the script and ask the lead: *am* I here for the right reasons?

The drama with Kupah doesn't end there. He mouths off loudly about their conversation to the other men, and Kaitlyn decides she's had enough and sends him home. After being a bit of a shit to Kaitlyn, Kupah then gets into a drunken spat and yells at a producer in his exit interview:

You don't even know me, man! I'm not a part of this thing, I'm not about this thing. This is bullshit. I do think your process works for some people like Jared and Cupcake, you know what I'm saying? But not me.

Just ask me the questions and let me go home, dude. Please. Please just give me that. What, I'm upset I didn't get a rose, I'm upset she sent me home, I'm upset there's no connection. Whatever!

And here something is edited out — a question the producer asks Kupah, maybe. Whatever it is, Kupah yells in response: "I lose immediately! Come on, man. Immediately I lose. Immediately. I lose! I lose." He paces away from and back towards the camera in a way that's vaguely threatening. He's making a scene. Kaitlyn emerges to shut it down and looks like a baller doing it.

There are two ways to read Kupah's outburst. One is that he's a dude having a hissy because a woman has denied him something he wants. (When Kaitlyn sends him packing, his big appeal to stay is "I don't want to go home: I think you're hot, I think you're sexy, I think you're pretty." Kaitlyn is understandably a little less than charmed.) And honestly, that's probably, at least partially, the case. But that reading doesn't exclude this one: Kupah is articulating what it's like to be a Black man in a position in which historically only white people have thrived. He tried to ask whether he was ever really welcome on the show, but found there were no words with which to do so, and the fact of the attempt got him canned. Kupah's shot at achieving *Bachelor*-romantic fluency is done. So now he's right: he's not a part of this thing. Immediately, he loses.

In the absence of *Bachelor*-ready coded ways to ask questions about race, contestants do sometimes resort to the un-ciphered version. In the second episode of Sean Lowe's season of *The Bachelor*,[96] for example, contestant Robyn tells producers: "I have noticed that the show is becoming more culturally diverse, so I am actually interested in getting to know what exactly he's looking for and how race plays into it . . . I'm not completely and totally sure Sean's attracted to Black females."

So Robyn sits down with Sean and tells him he might want to take off his jacket because she has a question that might get a nervous sweat going.

ROBYN: I was watching how [the show] became more diverse. With people. With ethnicity . . .

SEAN: I love this question, by the way. I already know where it's going . . . Let me tell you. This is the best question I've had all night. I love this question

96 This season was, not-so-coincidentally, the first to air post–class action.

. . . People look at me: blond hair, blue eyes, and they assume he probably goes for white girls who are blond. Honestly, physically, I don't have a type . . . I've dated everybody. And when I say everybody, I mean Hispanic, Persian. My last girlfriend: Black. I don't really have criteria. It's the mind and it's the woman behind the physical appearance.

ROBYN: Your answers are so perfect I can't take it sometimes.

Sean, again, reiterates how much he loved getting to speak to this topic. "I don't think he cares about color," Robyn tells producers in an ITM. "I'm so much more relaxed with you now," she tells Sean.

But Robyn probably shouldn't relax. When she goes home three weeks later, it's because she gets into a confrontation with another contestant. Never mind that the contestant Robyn has it out with is the season's villain, whom no one likes and several different women stage confrontations with; when the time comes, Robyn is the only one left holding the bag.

As soon as Kupah raises the issue of tokenism, he is shown to be irrational and even potentially violent, so when Kaitlyn tells him to leave, the audience can feel that she's justified in doing so. Kaitlyn never really hears Kupah's concerns; his role in her journey is to reveal her as someone with a backbone and a sense of clarity. He makes the Bachelorette look good, and then he's made into a Black stereotype. Similarly, the show gives

Robyn room to address race with Sean so that he can giddily declare his (and by extension the show's) keen, good-natured tolerance. Having played her role, Robyn is now disposable.

The franchise uses Black contestants to air racial grievances in ways that cultivate an appearance of openness and honesty on the show's part, only to then let these contestants take the fall, sometimes on the grounds of stereotypes that are, in themselves, racially charged. To the extent that Black contestants are featured in the show's narrative at all, they're more likely to show up in dramatic, confrontational B-plots than to be at the center of any love stories.[97]

The way the show uses Black characters to make itself look good is never more cleverly or heinously performed than in the treatment of Jubilee Sharpe on Ben Higgins's season of *The Bachelor* in 2016. Jubilee, a U.S. Army soldier and Haitian orphan, was characterized by Lauren H. (someone blond and forgettable) as implicitly unfit to be friends with "the other soccer moms"[98] in Ben's future nuclear familial life. Jubilee also committed the unpardonable sin of joking that someone else could take her date for her, since it involved a helicopter and she was nervous. According to a small but vocal group of that season's Stepford Wifeys, this was unconscionably disrespectful to Ben, to the other women, to "the process." Basically, there was a half-hearted attempt to characterize

---

97 Rachel E. Dubrofsky makes this point in her 2006 academic article "Whiteness in the Harem," examining how in the show's earliest seasons, women of color are used to centralize romance for white people. Though the article is more than a decade old, the trends Dubrofsky identifies have remained.

98 Lauren pronounces this "maaaaams" in a particularly aggressive Midwestern way.

Jubilee as a villain, which sort of sputtered out because of how much of a goddamn champion she was, and how obviously she was just doing her own thing, not well versed in the show's sycophantic social demands.

Then came "The Women Tell All." The role Jubilee played in the house dynamic was up for rehashing, with the women given the chance to criticize her demeanor and behavior on the show.[99] Contestants Jami and Amber, who are seated side-by-side with nearly identical haircuts, have this to say:

JAMI: I can speak for me and some other people that are biracial —

AMBER: [*laughs, raises her hand*] Just me! It's just me!

JAMI: [*to Jubilee*] You had said on numerous occasions that I'm here, I'm the real Black girl, I'm going to make it the furthest for a full Black woman.

. . .

AMBER: You said these little comments to us [*gestures to herself and Jami*] and I would take offense to it. Hearing the n-word, or hearing you're not Black enough — that hurt.

---

99 Which is standard for "The Men/Women Tell All," not anything specific to Jubilee.

Jubilee, for her part, denies these incidents: "I might have said I was bringing some diversity, but I would have never said I'm the real Black girl on the show." But regardless of what was or was not said, the point is that the show is talking in an open way about race, but making it into the Black women's problem. In fact, they're making the Black women *themselves* into the problem. The show doesn't even see race, this suggests — only *they* do. *The Bachelor* doesn't have a race problem — Jubilee does.

But wait, there's more. Now tagged as the most racist person in the room, Jubilee is then invited to sit in the hot seat for a chat with Chris Harrison. And here the tone shifts: Harrison's interview and the montage that accompanies it are pitched to maximize sympathy for Jubilee, reminding us of the deep trauma in her past,[100] encouraging her to air her orphan's fear of being "hard to love." The camera cuts away again and again to the women onstage and in the audience, a barometer of white faces welling with empathy.

Chris Harrison tells Jubilee, "I hope you realize that a guy as terrific as Ben saw you and got you. If nothing else, I hope you realize that you are that person." When Jubilee mentions that she's still in the military, Harrison interrupts her to thank her solemnly for her service. The room cheers to her good old American heroism.

The Bachelor has performed an incredible feat of cathexis here. First riling blame and disgust with Jubilee for being

---

100 As Jubilee puts it: "That's not a basis for a romantic relationship: Hey Ben, my whole family died. Let's makeout."

the one to insist on racial difference, then, after a reversal, re-embracing Jubilee. Having offloaded its own race issues onto her, the show then forgives Jubilee — and, by extension, itself. Emotions stoked, attached, cleared away. An atrocious moment, masterfully produced.

In February 2017, as Nick Viall was rounding the corner on hometown dates, the franchise partially spoiled his season by announcing Rachel Lindsay (who was still, as far as viewers knew, in the running for Nick's hand), as the next Bachelorette.[101] Here it was: after 15 years and 33 combined *Bachelor* and *Bachelorette* seasons, the show had finally cast a Black lead.

As a choice for Bachelorette, Rachel was unimpeachable. The winsome Texan lawyer (like, a legit lawyer as opposed to a *Bachelor*-job-description-type one) is everything: smart, funny, gorgeous, well spoken. I'm not even kidding when I say I think she should consider running for Congress.[102] On Nick's "The Women Tell All," Rachel emerges in a dress of the color white people call nude, beaming her zillion-watt smile with its perfect, fragile gap, and the audience rushes to give her a standing O. The other women from Nick's season can't keep

---

101 Show sources let slip to media that the rationale for the early reveal was to jump-start the casting process and give the show time to drum up a house full of suitable men . . . a.k.a. to come up with some Black cast members.

102 She comes from political pedigree: her father, Sam A. Lindsay, is a Clinton-appointed federal judge.

their shit together;[103] they scream and catcall and derail Chris Harrison's interview to talk over one another in a rush to list all of Rachel's amazing qualities. "My girls are so excited for me," Rachel laughs. I'm not sure there's been a Bachelorette more beloved.

When Chris Harrison asks her to comment on her "historic" status as the first Black Bachelorette, Rachel's inner politician kicks in: "I feel very honored to be the person to represent an African American woman in this position. It's a lot on my shoulders, but I'm ready to take it on." She adds, "I don't want that to be the focus of my journey, but I'm happy to acknowledge it."

So, Rachel was great. Probably too great. Her season was going to be the best.

And then . . . it wasn't.

In Chapter 3, I posited that we are in the dawning age of a new *Bachelor* villain whose destructive urges have a kind of catholic incorrigibility — the particular kind of alternatingly erratic and targeted shit-disturbery born and raised in the age of the internet. This trend is embodied all too thoroughly on Rachel's season in villain Lee Garrett: a wannabe country singer[104] who turned out to be a *literal internet troll*

---

103 Mmmmkay, so not to throw unnecessary shade, but Danielle L. (a.k.a. DLo) is the only one whose smile looks just the teensiest bit grit-mouthed. Methinks I spy someone who had her eye on *The Bachelorette* until she met Rachel Lindsay.

104 Has any aspiring country music star on this show ever turned out to be a good dude? To harken back to villains past, Lee's kind of a Wes from Jillian's season crossed with Ben from Des's.

with a history of racist, misogynist, and otherwise uncreatively vile tweeting.

Lee's social media output was exposed only once the season was already airing, but what was publicized in real time was confirmed in Lee's behavior onscreen. He kept starting shit with the other men, then playing the southern gent[105] when they responded, making it seem as if they and not he were behaving irrationally. Take this conversation with Eric Bigger (who wound up being Rachel's second runner-up), where Lee is accounting for having talked shit about Eric to Rachel:

LEE: I have no reservations to tell you that I said that because . . . out of all the guys, you had the most to learn . . . You are a great, capable individual. You have so much potential. And you're an amazing person . . . I still love you to death, and I think you're an amazing individual, but hearing you yell the way you did at Iggy last night —

ERIC: — changed your perception. That's fine.

LEE: I love you to death . . .

ERIC: You keep saying that, you keep saying — I just feel like you're not being honest.

---

105 To me, Lee looks and sounds like he'd be cast as the sexually frustrated second-in-command Confederate in a Civil War flick.

LEE: I'm being straightforward. I still love you.

ERIC: Why do you keep *saying* that? I'm *confused* . . .
I just feel like you're bullshitting me right now.

LEE: You're just closed off. If you don't want to talk
anymore, that's okay.

Lee ends the conversation by giving Eric the "gotcha"
finger gun and a wink. With these patronizing appraisals of
Eric's emotional development and off-base declarations of
"love," Lee is straight-up gaslighting. It's super weird and
uncomfortable and enraging.

When this plot line finally peters out, Lee moves on to
stir the pot with single dad pro wrestler Kenny King. Lee
accuses Kenny of being "aggressive" and tells him, "You have
an unrealistic violent aspect about you." (Even as he calls Lee
a "snake," Kenny takes pains to speak with a soft, soothing
voice, allowing no room to mistake his demeanor for anything
but calm.)

Will, one of the other Black contestants, takes on the
super fun task of reasoning with Lee:

LEE: What he wants is power.

WILL: What he wants to hear from you is nothing.

LEE: Oh, I can't do that.

Lee is obviously hammered here, and maybe it's giving him too much credit to make much of what he says. And yet I find this brief exchange revealing. Lee's anxieties are about ceding power to Kenny, and yet the thing Kenny wants (as interpreted by Will) — to be free of Lee's attentions — is, for Lee, equally unacceptable. Thus, in these two brief lines of dialogue, Lee succinctly expresses one of the foundational illogics of white supremacy: this Black man will not have power, and I won't leave him alone until he doesn't. I will not give him anything, and I can't stand to give him nothing.

In the sober light of day,[106] Will again takes one for the team and continues to patiently educate Lee about the racial dynamics underlying his tiff with Kenny:

LEE: He was being aggressive. I was just being honest . . . tell me that's not aggressive. Tell me that was not aggressive.

WILL: [*laughing*] I'm not going to say the words, man!

LEE: But why? You know, if you're going to be honest.

WILL: When you call him aggressive, there is a long-standing history in this country of regarding Black men in America as aggressive in order to justify a lot of other things.

---

106 Actually, I think they might be drinking again, but Lee seems less shit-faced.

You can see the understanding pass over Lee's face when he clues into what Will is saying. But it's not the right kind of understanding:

LEE: Oh, so he's the man who gets mad and plays the race card in order to get away with everything he does because he can't control himself.

WILL: I don't think he meant to play the race card, I think he truly was offended . . . If I'm looking at it from an objective standpoint, the way he's interpreting it, it is a very negative and potentially racially charged connotation.

To producers, Will explains his decision to help Lee educate himself: "It's probably something that Lee's never faced before. You know, it's not a part of his kind of experience growing up. It's probably a lot due to just ignorance on his part on how certain words can really trigger people."

That's generous, but Lee is not a good student. What he takes from his conversation with Will is that Kenny has something that he, Lee, does not: "When it comes to Kenny and his view on the world, I just don't understand it. I don't understand the race card, but it got played. Apparently."

As for the cards in Lee's own deck, his trumps are all troll: "I get tickled when I smile and an angry man gets angrier," he says. A fundamentally antisocial way to approach other human beings to begin with, what's worse is that Lee is getting his jollies only by provoking the Black men in the house. "I love getting under his skin," Lee says of Kenny, using a metaphor that's perhaps more telling than he realizes.

As Dean, another white contestant, puts it to a producer: "The only people that I've seen Lee pick fights with have been not the people that, uh, he's used to seeing on a daily basis, from a cultural perspective." "What do you mean by that?" the producer asks. "You know exactly what I mean when I say that," Dean throws back.[107]

For his part, Kenny appraises Lee thusly: "He's an alternative facts piece of garbage."

Lee's presence on the show was a major bummer, serving only to inhale airtime that ought to have been Rachel's. And that's true of all villain plots on *The Bachelor* and *Bachelorette* — villains send up obstacles and hazards that serve to make the hero's true love ending all the more precious. But Lee's villainy didn't do that; its racist overtones escalated the nature of the role from unpleasant to appalling.

In the "Men Tell All" episode, the season's villain is usually taken to task for interpersonal crimes committed during filming, plus whatever new grievances have come to light over the show's airing. Had Lee been like any other villain, his ride on "The Men Tell All" would likely have focused on the low-key sadism betrayed by his ITMs. Instead, most of the episode is spent contending with his extracurricular, pre-filming Twitter life. As he did two years prior at Kaitlyn Bristowe's

---

107 Note, again, the show's lexical gap around race.

"Men Tell All," Chris Harrison calls up the offending tweets onto a screen, projecting the words large-scale for the audience's benefit, and reads them aloud. After breezing through a couple of gems in which Lee suggests that women are like dogs and posits that feminism and physical attractiveness are mutually exclusive,[108] Harrison then gets to the pièce de résistance: a quip in which Lee compares the NAACP to the KKK, applauding the latter for at least hiding "their racist-ass faces."

Kenny, interestingly, says that at the time his conflict with Lee "didn't feel like racism. Racism feels a certain way: it's insidious, there's vitriol to it . . . It wasn't that way." And because it didn't seem so much like racism at the time, what Kenny and his cohort want to know is simply: Who *is* Lee? Where does the Twitter persona end and the man begin?

Lee's answers are prepared and empty and frustrating: "I should have been a better friend," and "I wasn't as considerate as I could have been in a lot of ways." The men use different strategies to goad Lee into breaking through his meaningless language. Josiah asks Chris Harrison for permission to approach the hot seat, sits beside Lee and asks him this:

> I want you to articulate to all of us: why did you come on a show where the Bachelorette was an African American woman if on the other hand you're tweeting

---

108 These are just the ones Harrison addresses, but screencaps of Lee's Twitter (which has since been made private) also reveal dozens more that rail against Hillary Clinton, "minority privilege," and LGBTQ activism. There's also the suggestion that the Irish were slaves in America (they weren't) and an endorsement of a petition to name Black Lives Matter a terrorist group.

about Black people and groups of Black people who fought and died so I can be on the stage next to you? People came before me so that I can go to the same school like you, so I can drink from the fountain like you. If you're comparing them to the KKK — people who hung my ancestors — why are you trying to date a woman who looks like me?

By sitting down beside him, Josiah makes himself undeniable to Lee. He's using his own body — his literal physical presence — as evidence of Black survival. He's talking in a very real way about life or death.

Lee — who, if his Twitter output is anything to go on, thinks that racism is a Bad Thing that happens to white people too — tells Josiah, "I don't like racism at all. It bothers me morally, it bothers me inside." He claims that this tweet lacks context, that it's a repost from Facebook that was cut off halfway through. But what context could possibly explain these words? As one of the men points out, Lee keeps talking about what his intention wasn't, and here he has an opportunity to explain what it was. What did he mean to say?

Lee doesn't answer. He continues to speak around something, talking about "things that I can learn, and things that a lot of people can learn." "Speak it! Speak it!" Anthony calls to him from the stage. Eventually, Anthony stands up to address Lee, to orate to the room:

Lee, I understand where you're coming from, but I

feel like you haven't acknowledged exactly what we're trying to forgive you for. I think you're just saying "I've been a bad person," but you're not acknowledging the invisible racism in your mind. You may not be doing it intentionally, but I think [it is] still motivating your actions. The racism that is ingrained in your behavior to the point of invisibility is still pushing you to behave in a certain way towards Eric, towards Kenny, towards me in a way that you don't even recognize. So, where are you now? Are you acknowledging that, even if you didn't intend it — are your actions motivated by racist thoughts that are implicitly embedded in your mentality?

Anthony gets a standing ovation. "That's a real question," he adds. After congratulating Anthony for being well-spoken (thanks, buddy), Lee concedes, "I did things that are wrong." "Wrong in what specific way?" Anthony presses. "You have to acknowledge that. You have to acknowledge it."

Here I think back to the moment earlier in the season when Lee wanted Will to say Kenny was "aggressive" and thus confirm his own worldview, but Will, who knows quite precisely the value of speech, was "not going to say the words." Now here's Lee, facing the power words have to give form to something insubstantial. Eventually, after much coaching, Lee finally points to the words written on the screen beside his name and says, "That tweet is racist, and I denounce it."

It's compelling to see avatars brought to life and brought

to account: that transition from abstract to concrete, from the simplicity of hatred to the complexity of something more human. This moment of crisis between Lee and the other men is very, very watchable. The frustration it gives rise to is a kind of suspense. Again and again Lee's face and body register struggle as he squirms away, letting himself off the hook, recycling platitudes about learning and friendship, turning to new justifications when these ones run thin. His apparent urge to protect himself surfaces so many times and seems so intractable that it starts to look almost like a kind of dissociative fugue — as if he might really not be certain whether or not he *is* the same person who wrote these tweets. Lee can't name the thing he's looking right at. Not racist, he says, but inconsiderate; not racist, incomplete. Not a racist — bad friend.

I don't just find this scene fascinating — I think it has the potential to be useful. Not in Lee's limited and obtuse concession, but in how hard he works to dodge making it. Even for those of us who have never taken to social media to express disgusting and ignorant thoughts, Lee's performance here should be read as cautionary. These are the mechanisms and failsafes deployed by a desperate ego in a tailspin — and they're actions any one of us might be capable of when trying to hold unpleasant self-knowledge at bay. And I think that's true for anyone in principle, but what I'm talking about right now are people who look Lee, and like myself. I'm talking about white people. I think it's worth watching Lee quite carefully here.

This whole scene is more about 2017 than it is about *The Bachelorette*, but its appearance on this particular show isn't merely incidental. After all, *The Bachelor* trades on a version of the Romantic that posits that great truths are those that are felt, not reasoned. That truth is affect, not evidence. Likewise, one of the biggest obstacles to racial reconciliation in America, I think, is a common misunderstanding on the part of white people that bigotry is something you feel, not what you do or say. In a way, white America's most banal racism is a kind of Romance — an attachment to the belief that tolerance is a matter of the heart.

In the end, Lee takes many tries to cop to very little. He goes so far as to recognize the literal words looming on the screen in front of him, but he's nowhere close to hearing Anthony's suggestion that he start combing his mentality for what is not immediately visible, start looking for evidence of that which he has not yet seen.

Admitting "that tweet is racist" isn't much, but the men onstage take it. Anthony says, "This is a growing experience for everybody . . . I want to help you out." Later, Rachel offers to give Lee a Black history lesson. Kenny talks about his young daughter and leading her by example into a world that is forgiving. "The way is forward," he says. "If you're willing to take that step . . . I am willing to stand along with my brothers and help you do so."

Truly, these are beautiful sentiments. But this is also about where I stop reading this whole situation as fascinating or instructive and start to feel pretty gross about what the show has pulled off. Because of course Lee never should have been on this show to begin with — shouldn't have been even nominally presented to Rachel Lindsay as someone to consider marrying. Whether producers vetted his social media closely enough to have known about the specific tweets at hand, certainly they knew *exactly* who Lee was and cast him for his potential to be "controversial." And now they're double-dipping on controversy: having spent weeks turning racism into entertainment, they compel our attention with a *mise en scène* in which racism is deconstructed and — the show would have us believe — dissolved. Even worse, the work of this deconstruction falls on the show's Black cast: Will patiently educates, Josiah puts his body on the line, Eric rises above, Anthony speaks in perfect paragraphs. And the show exploits their willingness to participate in Lee's rehabilitation. "I think we got there with Lee tonight," Chris Harrison surmises. So, no worries, guys — *The Bachelorette* solved racism! Hugs all around.

The Bachelor has always been good at making a mess and then making it go away. I'm going to use an analogy that spoils a 30-year-old magic trick, so if you don't want any iota of mystery sucked out of your universe, I suggest you skip ahead. What *The Bachelor* does well is like David Copperfield making the Statue of Liberty disappear: the statue didn't move — the stage on which the audience sat slowly, imperceptibly rotated away until it was facing out into the dark. The thing we're looking for is looming behind us, just out of sight. By focusing our attention on what *The Bachelor* tells us is worth watching, staring at the place where it stages its magic, we fail to notice that *we* are what moves. This is how most illusions work: they don't happen to the world of things, they happen to us. While it has our attention captured, *The Bachelor* swings us all the way around, until Liberty and nothingness are one and the same — until we don't even know where we are.

The Bachelor does not encourage the emotions it stokes to float freely through its universe — it attaches them to people, and uses those people to tell stories that always stick their landing. And at its most powerful and at its best, I think there's something to *The Bachelor*'s narrative talents — a catharsis this show can provide that the millions of people who watch it are clearly hungry for. But in the context of race, not only what *The Bachelor* does, but how it does it has the potential to be really troubling. Because the tale of race in America is nowhere near closure, and many of us who are white are only just coming to understand what our role in the story really is. ("You have to acknowledge it," Anthony says.) This isn't the moment for happily ever after: it's time to keep saying the words.

Obviously, including Lee in Rachel's season was a real cockup. And there were other cringeworthy missteps on the part of both the show and its white contestants in the first, fumbling season of a Black Bachelorette: boy-band-pretty Dean introducing himself to Rachel with the line "I'm ready to go Black, and I'm never going to go back,"[109] or the group date rap battle (itself enough to kill by secondhand embarrassment)

---

109 You can tell this is a producer-planted line from the way Dean goes deer-like after he delivers it, like he doesn't know where the script goes from there. Rachel laughs gamely and totally takes it in stride because she is the champion of everything.

in which Peter freestyles about how Rachel is a "girl from the hood." (She's the daughter of a high-ranking judge.)

But the season was not *all* bad as far as its depiction of race is concerned. For one thing, if you were to apply the racial equivalent of a Bechdel Test[110] and tally up the number of times people of color who are fully realized as characters[111] talk about something other than white people, this season would make the grade. Like the Bechdel, that's not really a measure of how progressive a cultural product is — it's just the lowest barrier to *not* being actively damaging and retrograde. But this season did more, I think, than merely meet the minimum: never bolsters for other, whiter love stories, both Rachel and her Black suitors were consistently depicted as real and complete. And for the most part,[112] these men delivered a version of Black masculinity you rarely get to see on TV: fraternal, sensitive, family-oriented, with non-racially-stereotyped careers and long-term goals. That shouldn't feel like a breath of fresh air, but it does. And as for Rachel: we got to see a Black woman be in control. She got to make out with as many guys as she wanted, tell them to go away when she was done with them, and close the journey with a fairytale finish. She got exactly what this show provides.

It's frustrating to report that the show's ratings took a hit

---

110 Film critic Manohla Dargis of the *New York Times* has proposed that this should be called the DuVernay Test, after film director Ava DuVernay.

111 I mean relatively speaking — to the extent that any characters are fully realized on this show.

112 The exception being DeMario.

this season, eroding around a million viewers compared to the last round of *The Bachelorette*. I can't help but think — I *want* to believe — that the downtick reflects the show's mistakes in handling their first Black lead, not the (correct) choice to cast her in the first place. And I feel it's important to add that from a critical standpoint, this season proved that having a more diverse cast isn't just a way to win woke points or to stay out of what ABC might perceive as PC crosshairs: it's good for the show *as a show*.

Roll back to the previous year's *Bachelorette* with JoJo Fletcher. This was peak homogeneity: a crop of dudes who seemed like they'd all emerged from a single egg sac with identical, mousse-gobbling fades.[113] Their lack of distinguishing features was the stuff of memes, and the question that weighed most heavily upon the group was, quite literally, who had lately consumed the most meat. The jostling of these low-key clones was rarely fun or interesting to watch.

A concentrated dose of white bread isn't just boring because it's boring, but because it deprives the show of stakes. When all roads arrive at a facsimile of the same answer, the lead's choices — and the implicit undercurrent of fate that guides them — risk revealing themselves to be thin and arbitrary. Rachel's choices, by comparison, have greater consequence because her suitors are distinguishable as individual humans. If anything, the fact of diversifying the show after so long risks making Rachel's particular choices between

---

113 A lil extra gobble on the top for Jordan Rodgers, please.

individual men seem *too* important — a referendum on dating Black vs. dating white.

Which brings us to the depiction of interracial dating itself. To harken back to *UnREAL* again for a second, in that universe, *Everlasting* producers don't plan to use their first Black lead to dispel backward dating taboos, but to exploit interracial optics: "I promise you 20 million viewers the minute he lays Black hands on a white ass. Twitter will melt down," Quinn tells a network exec. Quinn knows that the Hays Code[114] lingers even now, and she plans to capitalize on a perceived white audience's latent fears and fantasies of "miscegenation."

Crass and horrifying as Quinn's view here is, I wouldn't have been surprised had *The Bachelor* followed suit. But in fact, on Rachel's season (and Nick Viall's, for that matter[115]) interracial romance is treated about as thoughtfully as this show has ever treated anything. We are privy, for example, to conversations between men discussing whether race plays into Rachel's choices, and ones where they discuss whether and how to reveal the racial makeup of their own dating histories. In one instance, a Black contestant admits to Rachel that he's mostly dated white girls — a fact that appears to influence her decision to send him home. In another scene, Rachel pauses in the

---

114 A.k.a the Motion Picture Production Code: guidelines adopted in the 1930s to regulate the depiction of "immorality" in film.

115 On her hometown date, for example, Rachel's family gives just the right amount of humor and realness about interracial coupling. Rachel's sister and mother speak calmly and frankly about societal racism and a changing political climate, while Rachel's white brother-in-law jokes to Nick, "I can't help but notice: you are a white." It's fantastic.

middle of making out to ask a date with Colombian heritage whether his family will "accept" her. The kinds of questions and concerns that might arise between couples of mixed race aren't elided, but they also aren't exploited. In a way that really *is* dramatic for the *Bachelor* franchise, they're just . . . depicted.

Let's talk about how Rachel's season ended. At a glance, the season came to a close as it is wont to: the Bachelorette standing before a foreign panorama looking like she's been dipped in sequins while her winning suitor takes a knee and, under duress of less-than-ideal weather (in this case a mic-harassing wind beating against the Spanish cliff on which they're perched), he whips out the Neil Lane monstrosity of his choosing. He asks; she answers; they kiss. It was just like it always is, just like it's supposed to be.

But also not. As Rachel's finale ground down to happily ever after, Bachelor Nation took to Twitter in disgust, making declarations of horror and disappointment, sending out end-less gifs, references to election night 2016, etc. The problem, according to fans, was not how, but with whom: Bryan Abasolo, a 37-year-old chiropractor (he calls himself a "chiropractic phy-sician") from Miami who was unburdened by doubt, totally unflappable in his pursuit of Rachel. Which is fine, I guess, but onscreen, the smooth surface of Bryan's certainty looked dis-ingenuous — skeevy and sort of pointlessly slick — and every time he and Rachel kissed we were offered a reminder of where the expression "sucking face" comes from. Plus, to be honest, his relationship with his mom vibed a little womb-adjacent for my taste. But Rachel liked him straight off.[116] No one else could see it. Or maybe we just didn't want to.

As a Rachel Lindsay enthusiast, I found this conclusion tough to take at the time. But as a *Bachelor* scholar (I wouldn't say "*Bachelor* physician," but hey, someone might), I know that it was right and true. Because Rachel's ending is the natural outcome of a show that has always pretended to be about the production of fantasy, but is really about how people make do — how they maintain the scraps of their humanity, how they make difficult life choices — under inadequate conditions.

Bachelor Nation's Twitter horror was so piqued because for most of the finale, the camera wasn't aimed at Rachel's now-fiancé, but on a second choice who pulled up lame: fan favorite Peter Kraus — a 31-year-old Wisconsinite "business owner"[117] — who looks the way ads for Scotch and watches too fancy to be called watches (they're *timepieces*) would like to trick middle-aged men into thinking they appear.

As they near decision-making time, Rachel and Peter come to their relationship's final impasse: she wants to get engaged (duh, she's the Bachelorette), and he doesn't (yet). His plan, allegedly, is to defer a proposal and give the relationship time to develop off-camera before they commit. What he has in mind is still a fantasy, but in a lower key than the one *The*

---

116 Bryan received the first impression rose, making Rachel the third Bachelorette in a row to pin the eventual winner on night one.

117 He's really a trainer, but on a season with too many fitness pros in the running, he was slapped with a more serious-sounding job title.

Bachelorette provides: he wants a lazy Sunday morning kind of love, with farmers markets and handholding. Brunch first, diamond ring later.

But Rachel isn't having it — she didn't go through the *Bachelorette* wringer in order to come out the other side with just some boyfriend. (I'm sure dudes who want to date the shit out of her are a dime a dozen.) Rachel wants love and romance and a legally binding contract (again: fair enough, she's the Bachelorette). And so, Peter and Rachel say their first I love you's, share a tearful makeout, and break up for good. Rachel weeps the fake eyelashes right off her face and onto the floor where, apparently, Peter steps mournfully over the memento for several days.

Onscreen, Rachel segues from a moment so raw her body appeared to literally reject the façade of false lashes to a cliffside proposal that looked garish and hollow. Until now, it seemed as if Rachel could do no wrong, and yet here she was, giving it away to a guy no one could stand. "We're engaged!" Rachel screams to the Rioja peaks. In a few short moments, Rachel Lindsay went from a Bachelorette everyone loved to one half of a *Bachelor* couple no one wanted to contemplate.

As I've written elsewhere in this book, being the Bachelorette is hard. The job twines playing the heroine on an entertaining TV show and actually falling in love. These demands are often in tension with one another, and the role requires either incredible emotional control, deep wells of denial, or both. The Bachelorette must transition quickly between being totally honest, suppressing her true feelings, and outright lying to people's faces. Factor in the surveillance and lack of sleep, and the gig sounds, to me, like a true nightmare.

And because the show waited so unconscionably long to reach what should have been a low-key milestone on the path towards racial equality, the pressure on Rachel's experience as Bachelorette was exponential. In addition to all the usual franchise scrutiny, Rachel faced that which comes from being the first person of color to occupy *any* position that has historically been held by an unbroken string of white people. So, besides the fact that she had to be twice as qualified and four times as classy to even sit where she was, Rachel also had to consider how her decisions would be perceived by two audiences, each with different investments in her journey's outcome. Rachel is the only Bachelorette who's ever had to think not only about what she wants, but about what her desires *look* like.

Exhausted, Rachel tells a producer in an ITM, "You don't understand the pressures that are going to come with all of this . . . I'm going to get emotional. The pressures that I feel about being a Black woman and what that is and how — I don't want to talk about it." Rachel is no dummy: she knows exactly who will bear the consequences of her choices: "I already know what people are going to say about me, and judge me for decisions I'm making. I'm going to have to be the one who deals with that, and nobody else, and that's a lot . . . You have no idea what it's like to be in this position," she says. "I don't. I don't at all," the disembodied producer agrees. "I'm not talking anymore," Rachel says, exercising her only real bargaining power: to stop providing language.

To be clear: Rachel Lindsay was a fantastic Bachelorette. She was graceful and funny and a hardass when she needed to be. She kept her shit together while also giving us moments of truly great TV. When the season seemed like a bummer (the far-too-many minutes spent on Lee), or a slog (the long stretches when it seemed like every one of her suitors might be an unsuitable dud), Rachel kept up her shine. And then she made a choice we might not have liked, but which was the natural conclusion of the show we'd always been watching — one that purports to deliver the fantasy of romance, but is really about the pragmatism of choice.

It bears noting that Rachel is not the first Bachelorette who, from the outside, appeared to compromise in order to get her big moment and her big rock. Back in 2013, Bachelorette Des Hartsock was rounding the corner on the final rose when her far-and-away front-runner, Brooks, admitted that he wasn't exactly super into the idea of marrying her. They held one another, shared an ugly cry, and said goodbye. By the end of the next episode, her face still bearing traces of a sobfest, Des was engaged to someone else. And thus the Bachelorette didn't end up with the one she'd fallen hardest for, but the one she shared a passionate interest with: using the limited foundation provided by a reality TV show as the basis for a real-life commitment. They're still married, have a kid, and seem like about as normcore a couple as the show has ever produced.

I think we need to believe Rachel when she says (as she snapped at Peter when they confronted one another live at the airing of the finale) that she is now "living [her] best life." This season won't have made up any ground at all unless we allow Rachel the outcome that was always hers — the foregone conclusion of the show we all signed on to watch. Because isn't that, in a way, what equality actually means — the freedom to make self-actualizing choices even if they might turn out to be crappy ones? Not needing to be exceptional in order to have one's humanity recognized?

I kind of lied earlier when I said there's no *Bachelor* word for Black. Rachel's season was billed as an "historic" one — which makes for a pretty classic *Bachelor* euphemism, just with a limited shelf life. Because here's the thing about history: it's seen in "firsts," but felt in "seconds." Change isn't really about groundbreakers; it's the consequences of breaking ground. It's what happens when exceptions lose their shine, fade into norms. That dulling isn't a downgrade — it's a good thing. It means the chance for something to be special because it's special, not just because it's new.

I suspect that many of us in Bachelor Nation are possessed of a special kind of hypocrisy — one that affords complete immersion in a show we believe we are above. And because Rachel's so high caliber, we might have wanted to think of her as a proxy for that contradiction, wanted her to be the star of a show she was too good for, and still deliver an ending that would make *us* feel good. But Rachel Lindsay was no more too good to be the Bachelorette than any of us is too good to watch it, and what she wanted from the show was exactly what it provided: the chance to wear sparkles and diamonds and scream out her engagement from the top of a mountain. Of course she did. We wanted Rachel to be perfect; what we owe her is the right to choose mediocrity. Just like everyone. Just like all of us.

Conclusion: After the Final Rose

You may have noticed that a not-insubstantial portion of this book's ink has been spilled on the topic of "conditions." I've talked about those conditions *The Bachelor* produces to make its stories come to life. I've speculated about the cultural conditions into which those stories are projected — what changes sweeping through our lives and pictures and technologies have meant to the resonance of the show's telling and retelling.

This focus on the conditional stems from a premise so basic to how I think — such a no-brainer in my brain — that it didn't occur to me until late in the game that it might be helpful to state it outright: I've been assuming that art is exactly as impressionable as the people who make it, who consume it. That both the world in which a thing is made and the one into which it follows will leave their trace on what that something *is*. So if you're on a mission to look for meaning in a piece of cultural fabrication, the marks and prints left behind by context — any whorls and loops that might be visible to the naked eye — seem to me as good a place as any to start.

In July 2016, a few days before the Democratic and Republican National Conventions confirmed their respective candidates for president, I proposed a book of cultural criticism about *The Bachelor* to ECW's Pop Classics series. In my pitch, I argued that a fundamental contradiction baked into the show's generic structures almost addictively reflects a similar opposition at the heart of American identity. Love! Reality! U-S-A!

The project got the green light. In the fall, I started writing, and I refreshed my familiarity with *The Bachelor* canon. A stream of episodes running at a low constant under my life, spilling inside the lip of my conscious attention anytime I did anything in which attention is roughly divisible. I cooked, cleaned, and did burpees to the tune of *The Bachelor*. I felt its logic enter through my pores. My dreams acquired a kind of double vision, were narrated as they happened by some shifting, obscure In the Moment voice-over.

The weather was warm. I went for runs along the river near my house and through the shade of the city's Midwestern ravines, my ears budded shut while the voices of *Slate's Political Gabfest* narrated my mileage. I kept the *FiveThirtyEight* homepage open on my desktop. I recycled streams of numbers, trains of thought, prodding at any means of assurance that Hillary Clinton would succeed Barack Obama as president. Or, more to the point, that (duh) Donald Trump could not.

In September, the day after my 30th birthday, I propped my laptop in the hall outside the bathroom and streamed the first presidential debate while I cleaned my toilet.

While I wrote about fantasy suites and sex, Donald Trump bragged about grabbing women by the pussy. And from where I sat in my *Bachelor* marinade, the footage looked uncannily like a limo exit: car with tinted windows rolling up slowly, disembodied voices of the men inside cheering as they spot the pretty woman waiting for them at the end of the driveway, all done up in her nice dress. But in this version, the rhapsodic shouts are rapey humblebrags. And in this version, the contestant who opens the door and introduces himself with all the smarm of a crap season's villain-to-be was now a candidate to be the most powerful man in the world.

Like a lot of people did, I thought that this would be the end of Trump's run. And not even because of what he says behind the dark screen of the bus windows, but because of the part right after that, those seconds when he blinks into the light and sidles up for a handshake. The moment a gap cleaves between person and persona. It's not politics, or smarts, or the containment of multitudes: it's the boring, everyday distance between what you want and what you want other people to see. We all know it. No one likes to watch it happen.

In October, women came forward with more than a dozen allegations of sexual harassment against Trump. In October, it turned out it didn't matter. In October, I axed a chapter my book proposal had called "Finding Feminism on *The Bachelor*."

While I was writing about stories of American trauma, I got a text from the emergency alert system of the state university where I studied and taught saying there was an active shooter on campus. My phone said: *Run Hide Fight.*

And, of course, on November 8, 2016, I left my cursor at the end of a paragraph about villains who do not merely threaten their opponents, but troll the foundational structures of the universe in which they turn. The cursor was pulsing there the next morning, asking for more.

Mostly this: I planned to write a book about what a reality TV show tells us about America, and then, while I was writing it, a reality TV star became the American president.

The bulk of this short book was written during the fresh, crackling hangover between election and inauguration — the rest in the soggy dawn of the Trump presidency. During this time, I acquired some things and some habits.

I bought an app that lets you control when and how the internet can get into your computer and phone which is, I shit you not, called Freedom. Not a means of entering the world unfettered — it's a way to keep the world away. I spent $99 to buy back the privacy and quiet of my own mind.

I bought candles in bulk, lit amateur formations around my desk, and loved my work best like this: crouched in the dark, elemental light and heat larding the glow of the screen as I banged out words.

I woke earlier and earlier to write, looking for the thickest darkness I could find. I felt like I was crawling into a mouth, slipping down the back of a throat. Waking up at five became four became three a.m. I chased the morning until I found it right in the middle of the night.

I developed an oddly pleasant tingle at the base of my wrist that creeps in on the days I have burned myself out by typing. At 30, my knees started feeling weird, and I switched from running to yoga. I've been eating more meat, and eating it more rare.

I hypnotized myself on endless Spotify playlists devoted to focus. I tried to focus on the thing that was right in front of me.

I shuffled and turned over tarot cards before I started writing. I showed up to my desk every day and performed rituals of interpretation.

This was a time of magical thinking. On Twitter, it was a battle of prognostication, singular voices of prophecy against the low, lulling mumble incanting fine, normal, and alright. Sitting at my desk, I tried my own hand at casting spells, casting prayers, and wondered whether American optimism might not be a fatal disease.

When I started writing this book, fake news wasn't a thing, and already it has cycled through a whole host of definitions and landed on that which belongs to whoever yells loudest.

Every day for the last year, it seemed as though something new arrived, some image or word by which one is forced to recalibrate not only a sense of moral clarity, but a more basic, factual understanding of what is real.

Every day is the most dramatic ever. The most dramatic yet.

In the same month that Donald Trump became the 45th President of the United States, Nick Viall became the 21st Bachelor, fulfilling his remarkable turn from villain to hero, ending one quest narrative with the start of another. Before Nick was cast, the show had prepped, locked, and loaded Luke Pell, an army vet with country music aspirations. It was a classic choice — one for the heartland. One day Luke was it, and the next day he just wasn't. By swapping in Nick at the 11th hour, the *Bachelor* elected to cast a lead who is deeply versed in the system and nonetheless threatens to disrupt it. He was the too-clever-by-half insider *and* the superficial reality star.

I was concerned that the task of producing Nick might top *The Bachelor* out, sail it over the edge of its zenith. I should have known better than to worry. *The Bachelor* once again made itself accommodating *through* stubborn persistence, insisting that its improbable logic can endure just about anything — even the journey of its own coming-to-self-conscious creation.

And Nick begat Rachel Lindsay. We said goodbye to the era of Obama and got our first Black Bachelorette.

I wrote this book under conditions you will know as the past. I wrote it in Columbus, Ohio: a place where corporations come to test their products, feeling for the quintessential, predictive pulse of the American consumer. After nearly three years of living in the United States — nine seasons' worth of *Bachelor* — I'm going home to Canada, just in time to drink of *Paradise*.

I will be the first to admit I have had moments of crisis while writing this particular book at this particular moment. There have been times when this project has seemed worryingly frothy, and I've wondered whether my energy and attentions might be more responsibly donated elsewhere. I am particularly lucky and particularly safe, and even so for the last few months I have felt as though I was looking into a maw of total doom I am not predisposed to recognize meaning in.

I also have to admit something far more embarrassing, but also more consistently true: this *Bachelor* apologia has been vital to me. It has felt like the only thing I could possibly be doing.

I mean, how stupid is that?

No, really, I'm asking.

All writing is a time capsule; it just feels like time is moving away from the present especially quickly right now. I'm trying to dip something in wax before the ends fray. Turnover and preservation: these are things *The Bachelor* has always understood better than the rest of us.

For months I have been asking again and again: what does it mean to live under false premises? What does it mean for a feeling to be real? Why are stories we tell about who we are and what we deserve more powerful than all evidence mounting to the contrary around us? Is that power a good thing? How far will our imaginations take us?

I'm not deluded enough to think that this book about *The Bachelor* has answered these questions. But I am just deluded enough to feel that the task of asking them has helped me exist at a time in which so many of my assumptions about existence have made themselves known. I guess I'm saying that everything is political *and* it's personal. We're capable of great suspensions of belief, capable of keeping such big contradictions in our minds.

If that by which we call a rose by any other name would smell as sweet, we can take this as an imperative to go into the world with our senses dialed towards appreciation, towards trust. Take it as a reminder to test our beliefs against the world we feel, not the one that is told to us. And if there's something unnerving buried in the adage too — the sense that the words we use to describe our truths might shift, or elude us, or be taken away — well, I think I'm more ready for that now.

If nothing else at all, *The Bachelor* has taught me this: under the right conditions, the very best and worst of us can be drawn out, put up for display, performed broadly. It's taught me that ceremonies matter. But also that anything can be a ceremony.

Outside it's probably day by now, but in here you wouldn't know it. The windows are covered by blackout curtains in fancy dress: overzealous, emergency-thick velour. We've been cut off from time, preserved in a room that looks like it's hosting a convention for home décor accessories, an homage to the dignity and self-sufficiency of the garnish.

Before the bricolage of Anthropologie castoffs, by the light of a zillion candles, he stands before the women staged on risers like a chorus. He lifts a single, long-stemmed rose — best on the faux-floral market — from a pile dwindling on the accent table, holds it in front of his chest, and breathes. He's waiting for the signal to make a choice, call a name, ask what they all ask.

And lately, when I picture what comes next, I tell myself to stop short of the end. The question isn't *Will you accept this rose?*

It's more like *Will you accept this —*

More like:

Will you accept this?

Selected Sources

"2006 Word of the Year." *Merriam-Webster*. 2006.

Abdul-Jabbar, Karim. "*The Bachelor* Is Killing Romance in America." *The Hollywood Reporter*. January 2, 2017.

"Blind Date (TV Series 1999–2006)." *The Internet Movie Database (IMDb)*.

Bricker, Tierney. "DeMario Jackson Issues Statement on *Bachelor in Paradise*: My Character Has Been Assassinated." *E! News*. June 14, 2017.

Brodesser-Akner, Taffy. "Chris Harrison: The Reigning King of *The Bachelor*." *GQ*. January 1, 2015.

Carbone, Gina. "Which *Bachelor* Season Had the Best Ratings?" *Wetpaint*. December 4, 2013.

Chozick, Amy, and Bill Carter. "After Rough Patch, *The Bachelor* Wins Back Viewers." *New York Times*. March 10, 2013.

Claybrooks v. American Broadcasting Companies. U.S. District Court for the Middle District of Tennessee. 2012. Civil Right Litigation Clearing

House. University of Michigan Law School.

"The Dating Game (TV Series 1965–1986)." *The Internet Movie Database (IMDb)*.

Dewey, Caitlin. "That Hoax Isn't Funny Anymore: Elan Gale and the Problem of Reality Online." *Washington Post*. December 3, 2013.

Dubrofsky, Rachel E. "Whiteness in the Harem." *Critical Studies in Media Communication* 26, no. 1 (March 2006): 39–56.

Dutton, Donald G., and Arthur P. Aron. "Some Evidence for Heightened Sexual Attraction under Conditions of High Anxiety." *Journal of Personality and Social Psychology* 30, no. 4 (1974): 510–517.

Fitzpatrick, Molly. "A History of Black Contestants on *The Bachelor* and *The Bachelorette*." *Splinter*. February 2, 2016.

Gale, Elan (@theyearofelan). *Twitter*.

Gay, Roxane. "The Marriage Plot." *New York Times*. May 10, 2014.

"Inside *The Bachelor*: The Stories Behind the Rose." *20/20*. ABC. 2010.

"Interview with Ali Fedotowsky." *A Drink With*. February 6, 2013.

Kelley, Seth. "*Bachelor* Host Chris Harrison Slams Lifetime's *UnREAL*: 'It's Really Terrible.'" *Variety*. July 28, 2015.

Langer, Eli. "This Man Is Hilariously Live-Tweeting His Flight-and-Feud with the Woman in #7A." *Storify*. November, 2013.

Martin, Douglas. "George Barrett, Tennessee Lawyer Who Fought Desegregation, Dies at 86." *New York Times*. August 30, 2014.

Max, D.T. "Confessional: On *UnREAL*, a Former Producer of *The Bachelor* Satirizes Her Experience." *New Yorker*. June 20, 2016.

"Mike Fleiss." *The Internet Movie Database (IMDb)*.

Nietzsche, Friedrich. *Thus Spoke Zarathustra: A book for Everyone and No One*. Trans. Thomas Common. New York: Penguin Classics, 1985.

Otterson, Joe. "Corinne Olympios Ends *Bachelor in Paradise* Investigation, Will

Not Return to Series." *Variety*. June 29, 2017.

Piester, Lauren, and Beth Sobol. "Drink Logs & On-Camera Consent: *Bachelor in Paradise*'s Vinny Ventiera Details the New Post-Scandal Rules for Season 4." *E! News*. July 30, 2017.

Poggi, Jeanine. "Coming Up Rosy: Inside the Business of *The Bachelor*." *Advertising Age*. October 12, 2015.

Porter, Rick. "Monday Final Ratings: *The Bachelor* and *Scorpion* Adjust Up, *Blindspot* and *After the Final Rose* Adjust Down." *TV by the Numbers*. Tribune Media. March 15, 2016.

Robertson, Courtney, and Deb Baer. *I Didn't Come Here to Make Friends: Confessions of a Reality Show Villain*. New York: Itbooks, 2015.

Rorty, Richard. *Contingency, Irony, and Solidarity*. Cambridge: Cambridge University Press, 2009.

"Sanderson Patrick Poe." *Tulsa World*. May 23, 2013.

"Sexual Violence: Facts at a Glance." *Violence Prevention*. Centres for Disease Control and Prevention. 2012.

Shakespeare, William, and Jill L. Levenson. *Romeo and Juliet*. Oxford: Oxford University Press, 2000.

Shapiro, Sarah Gertrude, and Marti Noxon, creators. *UnREAL*. Lifetime. 2015–.

Smith, Kyle. "TV's Reality Check." *People*. March 6, 2000.

Stone, Natalie. "Corinne Olympios Breaks Silence on *Bachelor in Paradise* Scandal: 'I Am a Victim.'" *People*. June 14, 2017.

Sullivan, Michelle. "How Columbus Became America's Test Market." *Columbus Monthly*. January 28, 2015.

"*Temptation Island* (TV Series 2001–2003)." *The Internet Movie Database (IMDb)*.

Yuan, Jada. "A History of *The Bachelor*, by the People Who Lived It." *The Cut*. January 4, 2016.

Acknowledgments: With That Being Said

Thanks to the editors of the *Los Angeles Review of Books* and *Partisan* for first giving me room to write about *The Bachelor*. Versions of parts of the essays "*Bachelor* Vernacular" and "Did Kaitlyn Bristowe Break *The Bachelorette*?" appear in this book. Thanks also to the editors at *Buzzfeed Reader*, particularly Rachel Sanders, for publishing excerpts in advance of publication.

To Angus Fletcher, from whom I definitely stole a sentence on which this whole argument hinges.

To my creative writing students at Ohio State for indulging all my *Bachelor* and America chatter, and for often being the reason I showed up and tried to be something better than I was.

To Crissy and Jen for getting it right away and for being as brilliant as you are fun to hang with — the kind of editors who know how to do lunch right. You guys made me feel totally supported. I never could have come up with this without your Pop Classics vision.

To everyone at ECW who has worked or will work on this book: thank you all.

To Michael, for Screencap Recapping, aiding and abetting my love of this show, and always showing such unflagging confidence in my ability to write about it.

To Noelle, for so many things I couldn't have done without: cave life, Monday nights, most other nights, days pacing up and down the mighty Olentangy. For Lakeview, for all of it — it was thanks to you.

To my family, and especially my parents, Ellen and Peter, who taught me that love and critical thinking are of equal value.

And to Andrew, for all the best parts. For the real thing.

Suzannah Showler is the author of the poetry collections *Thing Is* and *Failure to Thrive*. She is a 2017–18 Presidential Fellow at The Ohio State University. Her essays and cultural criticism have appeared in places like *Buzzfeed*, *Slate*, *Los Angeles Review of Books*, *The Walrus*, and *Hazlitt*.

Get the eBook free!*

*proof of purchase required

At ECW Press, we want you to enjoy this book in whatever format you like, whenever you like. Leave your print book at home and take the eBook to go! Purchase the print edition and receive the eBook free. Just send an email to ebook@ecwpress.com and include:

• the book title
• the name of the store where you purchased it
• your receipt number
• your preference of file type: PDF or ePub?

A real person will respond to your email with your eBook attached. And thanks for supporting an independently owned Canadian publisher with your purchase!